Rick Steves®

SNAPSHOT

Italy's Cinque Terre

CONTENTS

INTRODUCTION

This Snapshot guide, excerpted from my guidebook *Rick Steves Italy,* introduces you to my favorite stretch of the Italian Riviera. The Cinque Terre—literally "five lands"—is a charm bracelet of picturesque, traffic-free villages where you can melt into small-town Italy. Sit on the breakwater to enjoy the views, hike the scenic trails between the villages, and dine on a succulent seafood feast as you hear the roar of the surf. I've also included coverage of nearby Riviera destinations, including the beach towns of Levanto, Sestri Levante, the larger Santa Margherita Ligure, trendier Portofino, resorty Portovenere, and the workaday transportation hub of La Spezia.

To help you have the best trip possible, I've included the following topics in this book:

• **Planning Your Time,** with advice on how to make the most of your limited time

• **Orientation,** including tourist information (abbreviated as TI), tips on public transportation, local tour options, and helpful hints

• **Sights** with ratings:

▲▲▲—Don't miss

▲▲—Try hard to see

▲—Worthwhile if you can make it

No rating—Worth knowing about

• **Sleeping** and **Eating,** with good-value recommendations in every price range

• **Connections,** with tips on trains, buses, and driving

Practicalities, near the end of this book, has information on money, staying connected, hotel reservations, transportation, and more, plus Italian survival phrases.

To travel smartly, read this little book in its entirety before you go. It's my hope that this guide will make your trip more meaningful and rewarding. Traveling like a temporary local, you'll get the absolute most out of every mile, minute, and dollar.

Buon viaggio!

Rick Steves

THE CINQUE TERRE

*Riomaggiore • Manarola • Corniglia • Vernazza •
Monterosso al Mare*

Along a beautifully isolated six-mile stretch of the most seductive corner of the Italian Riviera lies the Cinque Terre (CHINK-weh TAY-reh)—five *(cinque)* small towns gently and steadily carving a good life out of difficult terrain.

Each village fills a ravine with a lazy hive of human activity—calloused locals and sunburned travelers enjoying the area's unique mix of Italian culture and nature. With a traffic-free charm—a happy result of their natural isolation—these towns are the rugged alternative to the glitzy Riviera resorts nearby. There's not a Fiat or museum in sight—just sun, sea, sand (well, pebbles), wine, and pure, unadulterated Italy. Choose a home base according to just how cut off you'd like to be from the outer world (see the "Cinque Terre at a Glance" sidebar).

Enjoy the villages, swimming, hiking, and evening romance of one of God's great gifts to tourism. While the Cinque Terre is now discovered (and can be unpleasantly crowded midday, when tourist boats and cruise-ship excursions drop by), I've never seen happier, more relaxed tourists. Given that the vast majority of the crowds are day-trippers, make a point to get the most out of those cool, relaxed, and quiet hours early in the day and in the evening.

This chunk of coast was first described in medieval times as "the five lands." In the feudal era, this land was watched over by castles. Tiny communities grew up in their protective shadows, ready to run inside at the first hint of a Turkish Saracen pirate raid. Marauding pirates from North Africa were a persistent problem until about 1400. Many locals were kidnapped and ransomed or sold into slavery, and those who remained built fires on flat-roofed

The Cinque Terre

To A-12 Autostrada
(Brugnato Exit)

To
Genoa

A-12

SP-1

To A-12 Autostrada
(Carrodano Exit)

Beverino

To
La Spezia
& Pisa

SP-566

2 Kilometers

2 Miles

SP-1

To
Sestri Levante,
Santa Margherita
& Genoa

Pignone

Levanto

SP-370

To New Town
(Fegina)

To Monterosso's
Old Town

SP-38

Pian di
Barca

SP-1

SP-63

These roads may be closed.
Inquire locally.

To
La Spezia
& A-12

Monterosso
al Mare   ❺

SANDY
BEACH

❹

Vernazza

Corniglia

❸   SP-51

CORNIGLIA STATION

Volastra

Ligurian

Sea

Manarola   ❷

VIA DELL'AMORE ♥

VIA
LITORANEA

To
La Spezia
& A-12

Riomaggiore   ❶

SP-370

To Portovenere

watchtowers to relay warnings—alerting the entire coast to immi-
nent attacks. The last major raid was in 1545.

As the threat of pirates faded, the villages prospered, catching
fish and cultivating grapes. Churches were enlarged with a grow-
ing population. But until the advent of tourism in this generation,
the towns remained isolated. Even today, traditions survive, and
each of the five villages comes with a distinct dialect and its own
proud heritage.

Sadly, a few ugly, noisy Americans give tourism a bad name
here. Even hip, young residents are put off by loud, drunken tourists.
They say—and I agree—that the Cinque Terre is an exceptional
place. It deserves a special dignity. Party in Viareggio or Portofino,
but be mellow in the Cinque Terre. Talk softly. Help keep it clean.
In spite of the tourist crowds, it's still a real community, and we are
its guests.

In this chapter, I cover the five towns in order from south
to north—from Riomaggiore to Monterosso. Since I still get the
names of the towns mixed up, I think of them by number: #1
Riomaggiore (a workaday town), #2 Manarola (picturesque), #3
Corniglia (on a hilltop), #4 Vernazza (the region's cover girl, the
most touristy and dramatic), and #5 Monterosso al Mare (the closest thing to a beach resort of the five towns).

ARRIVAL IN THE CINQUE TERRE

By Train: Most big, fast trains from elsewhere in Italy speed right past the Cinque Terre. (There are some exceptions: A few IC trains

go directly from Milan to Monterosso and from Pisa to La Spezia and Monterosso.) Unless you're coming from a nearby town, you'll have to change trains at least once to reach Manarola, Corniglia, or Vernazza.

Generally, if you're coming from the north, you'll change trains in Sestri Levante or Genoa (specifically, Genoa's Piazza Principe station). If you're coming from the south or east, you'll probably switch trains in La Spezia (change at La Spezia Centrale station—don't make the mistake of getting off at La Spezia Migliarina). No matter where you're coming from, it's best to check in the station before you leave to see your full schedule and route options (use the computerized kiosks or ask at a ticket window). For more information on riding the train between Cinque Terre towns, see "Getting Around the Cinque Terre," later.

By Car: If you're driving in the Cinque Terre (but, given the narrow roads and lack of parking, I wouldn't), see "Cinque Terre Connections" at the end of this chapter for directions. For parking, see the "By Car" sections in each village.

PLANNING YOUR TIME

The ideal stay is two or three full days; my recommended minimum stay is two nights and a completely uninterrupted day. Speed demons arrive in the morning, check their bags in La Spezia, ride a train to their starting point, take the five-hour hike through all five towns (depending on which trails are open), laze away the afternoon on the beach or rock of their choice, and zoom away on a high-speed evening or overnight train to somewhere back in the real world. But be warned: The Cinque Terre has a strange way of messing up your momentum. (The evidence is the number of Americans who have fallen in love with the region and/or one of its residents...and are still here.) Frankly, staying fewer than two nights is a mistake that you'll likely regret.

The towns are just a few minutes apart by hourly train or boat. There's no checklist of sights or experiences—just a hike, the towns themselves, and your fondest vacation desires. Study this chapter in advance and piece together your best day, mixing hiking, swimming, trains, and a boat ride. For the best light, coolest temperatures, and fewest crowds, start your hike early.

Market days perk up the towns from around 8:00 to 13:00 on Tuesday in Vernazza, Wednesday in Levanto, Thursday in

Cinque Terre at a Glance

▲**Riomaggiore (Town #1)** The biggest and most workaday of the five villages. See page 20.

▲**Manarola (Town #2)** Waterfront village dotted with a picturesque mix of shops, houses, and vineyards. See page 30.

▲**Corniglia (Town #3)** Quiet hilltop village known for its cooler temperatures (it's the only one of the five villages not on the coast), few tourists, and tradition of fine wines. See page 39.

▲▲▲**Vernazza (Town #4)** The region's gem, crowned with a ruined castle above and a lively waterfront cradling a natural harbor below. See page 43.

▲▲**Monterosso al Mare (Town #5)** Resorty, flat, and spread out, with a charming old town, a modern new town, and the region's best beaches, swimming, and nightlife. See page 67.

Monterosso, Friday in La Spezia and Santa Margherita Ligure, and Saturday in Sestri Levante. (Levanto, Sestri Levante, La Spezia, and Santa Margherita Ligure are covered in the next chapter.)

The winter is really dead—most hotels and some restaurants close from January to March. The long Easter weekend (March 25-28 in 2016), May, June, and September are the peak of peak periods—the toughest times to find rooms. July (when the heat keeps away many potential hikers) and August (vacation time hasn't started yet) can be surprisingly light. In spring, the towns can feel inundated with Italian school groups day-tripping on excursions (they can't afford to sleep in this expensive area).

For more information on the region, see www.cinqueterre.it.

CINQUE TERRE PARK CARDS

Visitors hiking between the towns on coastal trails need to pay a park entrance fee. You have two options: the Cinque Terre Trekking Card or the Cinque Terre Treno Multi-Service Card. Both are valid until midnight on the expiration date and include free Wi-Fi at train stations. Write your name on your card or risk a fine. The configuration and pricing of these cards is often in flux—be aware that the following details may change before your visit. Those under 18 or over 70 get a discount, as do families of four or more (see www.parconazionale5terre.it).

The **Cinque Terre Trekking Card** costs €7.50 for one day of

The Cinque Terre National Park: Peaks and Valleys

Founded in 1999, the Cinque Terre National Marine Park was intended to get everyone thinking creatively about how to improve the area for the good of nature, the local communities, and its many visitors. The park designation has brought with it plenty of good things: money (in the form of trail fees), new regulations to protect wildlife, park-sponsored information centers at each train station, shuttle buses to help hikers reach distant trailheads, and improved walkways, trails, beaches, breakwaters, and docks.

But, perhaps predictably, the system has been corrupted by power and money. A charismatic and visionary past park president, nicknamed "The Pharaoh," made great inroads before poisoning the process with cronyism, forcing him to leave office in disgrace. Frequent landslides cut off trails—the main reason many people come here—and repairs are excruciatingly slow. Local grassroots movements (including Save Vernazza—see page 56—and a ragtag crew of Manarolans who donated their time to clear a scenic trail) have arguably done more to promote and preserve the Cinque Terre than has the park, even with its substantial budget. The latest park president, a retired sea admiral, is determined to make the park work. But given this region's old-fashioned ways and recent history of bureaucratic failure, no one is counting on it.

Keep in mind that the Cinque Terre is a moving target. Don't be surprised if park details (including entrance fees, shuttle buses, information desks, and so on) have changed by the time you visit.

hiking or €14.50 for two days (covers trails and ATC shuttle buses plus a few other extras but does not cover trains; buy at trailheads and at most train stations, no validation required).

The **Cinque Terre Treno Multi-Service Card** covers what the Cinque Terre Trekking Card does, plus local trains from Levanto to La Spezia (including all Cinque Terre towns). It's sold at TIs inside train stations, but not at trailheads (€12/1 day, €23/2 days, validate card at train station by punching it in the machine). To break even with this card, you'd have to hike and take three train trips every day.

GETTING AROUND THE CINQUE TERRE

Within the Cinque Terre, you can connect towns in three ways: by train, boat, or foot. Trains are cheaper, boats are more scenic, and hiking lets you enjoy more pasta. From a practical point of view, you should consider supplementing the often frustrating trains with the sometimes more convenient boats. The Via dell'Amore trail between Riomaggiore and Manarola is a delight and takes just a few minutes (if it's open), making the train not worth the wait.

By Train

By train, the five towns are just a few minutes apart. Along the coast here, trains go in only two directions: *"per* [to] *Genova"* (the Italian spelling of Genoa), northbound; or *"per La Spezia,"* southbound.

Tickets: Most rides within the region cost about €2. These tickets are good for 75 minutes in one direction, so you could conceivably use one for a brief stopover. A 40-kilometer ticket is good for six hours in one direction (€4). Buy tickets at the train station at the ticket window or Cinque Terre park desk, or from machines on the platform. Be sure to validate your ticket before you board by stamping it in the green-and-white machines located on train platforms and elsewhere in the station. Conductors here are notorious for levying stiff fines on tourists riding with a good but unstamped ticket. You can buy several tickets at once and use them as you like, validating as you go. If you have a Eurail Pass, don't spend one of your valuable travel days on the cheap Cinque Terre.

Schedule: Trains run about hourly in each direction, connecting all five towns. Since the train is the Cinque Terre's lifeline, shops, hotels, and restaurants often post the current schedule, and many also hand out copies of it. I find the printed schedules tricky since certain departures listed are for only weekdays, only Sundays, and so on (check the key carefully). Rather than rely on printed schedules, locals stop by the station and check the real-time TV monitors to see the next departure time—these are the best, most current source.

Important: Any train stopping at Vernazza, Corniglia, or Manarola is going to all the towns. Trains from Monterosso, Riomaggiore, or La Spezia sometimes skip lesser stations, so confirm that the train will stop at the town you need.

At the Platform: Convenient TV monitors posted at several places in each station clearly show what times the next trains in each direction are leaving (and, if they're late—*in ritardo*—how many minutes late they are expected to be). On the monitors, northbound trains are marked for *Genova, Levanto,* or *Sestri Levante;* southbound trains are marked for *La Spezia* or *Sarzana*. (Most northbound trains that stop at all Cinque Terre towns will list Sestri Levante as the *destinazione*.) To be sure you get on the right train, it helps to know your train's number and final destination.

Pickpocket Alert

At peak times the Cinque Terre can be notoriously crowded, and pickpockets dressed as tourists and locals aggressively and expertly work the most congested areas. Be on guard, especially in train stations, on train platforms, and on the trains themselves during any crush of people. Keep your things zipped up and buttoned down.

Assuming you're on vacation, accept the unpredictability of Cinque Terre trains—they're often late, unless you are, too, in which case they're on time. Relax while you wait—buy an ice cream or cup of coffee at a station bar. Scout the platform you need in advance, and then, when the train comes, casually walk over and hop on. This is especially easy in Monterosso, with its fine café-with-a-view on track #1 (direction: Milano/Genova), and in Vernazza, where you can hang out at the Blue Marlin Bar with a prepaid drink and dash when the train pulls in.

Getting Off: Know your stop. As the train leaves the town just before your destination, go to the door and get ready to slip out before the mobs flood in (making it impossible to get off). A word to the wise for novice tourists, who often miss their stop: The stations are small and the trains are long, so (especially in Vernazza) you might have to get off deep in a tunnel. Also, the doors don't open automatically—you may have to open the handle of the door yourself (twist the black handle, or lift up the red one). If a door isn't working, get a local's help or go quickly to the next car to leave.

Alternative: In calm weather, boats connect the towns about as frequently as the trains, though at different times; if you're in a rush, take whichever form of transport is leaving first.

By Boat

From Easter through October, a daily boat service connects Monterosso, Vernazza, Manarola, Riomaggiore, and Portove-nere. Though they can be very crowded, these boats provide a scenic way to get from town to town and survey where you just hiked. And boats offer the only efficient way to visit the nearby resort of Portovenere (see next chapter); the alternative is a tedious train-bus connection via  La Spezia. In peaceful weather, boats can be more reliable than trains, but if seas are rough, they don't run at all. Because the boats

nose in and tourists have to gingerly disembark onto little more than a plank, even a small chop can cancel some or all of the stops.

I see the tour boats as a syringe, injecting each town with a boost of euros. The towns are addicted, and they shoot up hourly through the summer. (Between 10:00 and 15:00—especially on weekends—masses of gawkers unload from boats, tour buses, and recently, cruise ships, inundating the villages and changing the feel of the region.)

Boats depart Monterosso about hourly (10:30-18:00), stopping at the Cinque Terre towns (except at Corniglia) and ending up an hour later in Portovenere. (Portovenere-Monterosso boats run 8:50-18:00.) The ticket price depends on the length of the boat ride (ranging from €4 for a very short ride between towns, to €10 between towns farther apart, up to €15 for a five-town, one-way ticket with stops; a five-town all-day pass costs €20). Round-trip tickets are slightly cheaper than two one-way trips. You can buy tickets at little stands at each town's harbor (tel. 0187-732-987 and 0187-818-440). Another all-day boat pass for €26 extends to Portovenere and includes a 40-minute scenic ride around three small islands (2/day). Boats are not covered by Cinque Terre park cards. Boat schedules are posted at docks, harbor bars, Cinque Terre park offices, and hotels (www.navigazionegolfodeipoeti.it).

By Shuttle Bus

ATC shuttle buses (which locals call *pulmino*) connect each Cinque Terre town with its closest parking lot and various points in the hills. The one you're most likely to use runs between Corniglia's train station and its hilltop town center. Note that these shuttle buses do not connect the towns with each other. Most rides cost €1.50 one-way (€2.50 from driver, free with Cinque Terre park card). You can ask about tickets and bus schedules at park info offices or TIs, or note the times posted at bus stops, but be aware that shuttle service is quite unreliable. Confirm the details carefully before planning your day around the bus. Note that shuttles may not run from 12:30 to 15:00, when they break for lunch. As you board, it's smart to tell the driver where you want to go. Departures often coordinate with train arrival times. Some (but not all) departures from Vernazza, Manarola, and Riomaggiore go beyond the parking lots and high into the hills. To soak in the scenery, you can ride up and hike down, or pay €3 for a round-trip ride (€5 on board) and just cruise both ways (30-45 minutes round-trip).

Hiking the Cinque Terre

All five towns are connected by good trails, marked with red-and-white paint, white arrows, and some signs. *Sentiero* means trail. The region has several numbered *sentieri,* but most visitors stick

Events in the Cinque Terre in 2016

For more festival information and to confirm dates, check www.cinqueterre.it and www.turismoinliguria.it. The food festivals in particular are subject to change.

March 27-28	All towns: Easter Sunday and Monday
April 25	All towns: Italian Liberation Day (stay away from the Cinque Terre this day, as locals literally shut down the trails)
May 1	All towns: Labor Day (another local holiday that packs the place mostly with day-trippers)
Mid-May	Monterosso: Lemon Festival
May 5	All towns: Ascension Day
Mid-June	Monterosso: Anchovy Festival
May 29	Monterosso and Vernazza: Feast of Corpus Domini (procession on carpet of flowers, second Sun after Pentecost)
June 24	Riomaggiore and Monterosso: Feast day of St. John the Baptist (procession and fireworks; big fire on Monterosso's old town beach the day before)
June 29	Corniglia: Feast day of Sts. Peter and Paul
July 20	Vernazza: Feast day of patron saint, St. Margaret, with fireworks
Early Aug (first Sun)	Vernazza: Feast of Nostra Signora di Reggio (hike up to Reggio Sanctuary for food and church procession)
Aug 10	Manarola: Feast day of patron saint, St. Lawrence
Aug 14	Monterosso: Fireworks on eve of feast of the Assumption
Aug 15	All towns: Feast of the Assumption (Ferragosto)
Mid-Sept	Monterosso: Anchovies and Olive Oil Festival

to the main coastal trail that connects the villages—that's trail #2 (described in the next section). For extra credit, get local advice for detours to dramatic hilltop sanctuaries. I've outlined my favorite non-#2 hike, from Manarola over Volastra to Corniglia, later.

Trail Closures: Trails can be closed in bad weather or due to landslides. Before planning your hiking day, carefully confirm whether any of the trail segments are closed. Official closures are noted on the national park website (www. parconazionale5terre.it) and are posted at the park-information desks in each town's train station. Very often a trail is "officially" closed—meaning that its ticket desk is closed—but still perfectly hikable (at your own risk). Ask locals or fellow hikers for the latest on which trails are actually passable and which aren't.

Hiking Conditions: Other than the wide, easy Riomaggiore-Manarola segment, the coastal trail is generally narrow, steep, rocky, and comes with lots of challenging steps. I get many emails from readers who say the trail was tougher than they'd expected. The rocks and metal grates can be slippery in the rain (I'd avoid the very steep Monterosso-Vernazza stretch if it's wet). Don't venture up on these rocky cliffs without sun protection or water. While the trail is challenging, it's perfectly doable for any fit hiker...and worth the sweat.

When to Go: The coastal trail can be very crowded (and very hot) at midday. The best times to hike are early in the day (before the crowds and heat hit) and late in the day. Before setting out for an evening hike, find out what time the sun sets, and leave yourself plenty of time to arrive at your destination before then; after dark, there's no lighting on the trails.

Navigation: Maps aren't necessary for the basic coastal hikes described here. But for the expanded version of this hike (12 hours, from Portovenere to Levanto) and more serious hikes in the high country, pick up a good hiking map (about €5, sold everywhere). The *Cinque Terre Walking Guide* (by a German publisher, but sold locally in an English-language edition for about €15) is worth seeking out for anyone planning a serious hike.

Give a Hoot: To leave the park cleaner than you found it, bring a plastic bag *(sacchetto di plastica)* and pick up a little trail trash along the way. It would be great if American visitors—who get so much joy out of this region—were known for this good deed.

Weather: As in many communities whose livelihoods are tied to the sea, locals have names for the different types of winds: *Scirocco* is a cloudy, warm, southeasterly wind from North Africa; it carries sand from the Sahara, which makes a mess as it scatters over the land. The *scirocco* causes a condition called *macaia*—sticky, heavy, wet, still, and overcast weather believed to put everyone in a rotten mood. Conversely, the *tramontana* is a cool, clear, refreshing, northerly breeze that comes "across the mountains," bringing sunny weather and calm seas. The *libeccio* wind, from the southwest (and named for Libya), means "sun but big waves." The *maestrale* is a stiff westerly that generally comes with sunny weather (and isn't as intense as France's notorious mistral). And *grecale* is a strong,

Cruise Ship Travelers Not Welcome in the Cinque Terre

In the past couple of years, cruise lines have begun offering Cinque Terre excursions from Livorno (the port for Florence) and have even been stopping in La Spezia specifically to tour the five towns. While cruisers have the right to enjoy every corner of the beautiful Mediterranean, it just makes no sense for cruise lines to dump literally thousands of travelers on a place like the Cinque Terre, which doesn't have the infrastructure for huge crowds. But by the nature of the cruise industry, it's either thousands or nobody; there's no middle ground. When the cruise ships are in, the Cinque Terre trails become almost impassable, and the towns' tiny main lanes become literal human traffic jams. Sure, those cruise travelers can then cross the Cinque Terre off their proverbial "bucket list." But nobody arriving with a cruise ship full of tourists can really experience the Cinque Terre. Locals don't like cruise tourists, and that feeling grows stronger every year. It's just a very bad scene. Please, visit on your own. But don't try to experience the villages and fragile trails of the Cinque Terre as part of a cruise ship mob. I love cruising. And I love the Cinque Terre. But in my *Rick Steves Mediterranean Cruise Ports* guidebook I barely mention the Cinque Terre. They just don't mix.

cold, northeasterly wind from Russia that produces chilly drizzle and sometimes snow in the mountains.

The Coastal Trail

As of late 2015, the hiking trail from Monterosso to Vernazza is open, the trail from Vernazza to Corniglia is perfectly passable but officially closed, and the trail from Corniglia to Manarola and to Riomaggiore (the famed Via dell'Amore) is closed and physically unpassable. Check locally for updates as trail conditions may change before your visit.

If all of the main trails are open, the entire seven-mile coastal hike (on trail #2, with lots of ups and downs between Corniglia and Monterosso) can be done in about four hours, but allow five for dawdling. Germans (with their task-oriented *Alpenstock* walking sticks) are notorious for marching too fast through the region. Take it slow...smell the cactus flowers and herbs, notice the scurrying lizards, listen to birds singing in the olive groves, and enjoy vistas on all sides.

If you're hiking the full five-town route, consider these factors: The trail between Riomaggiore (#1) and Manarola (#2) is easiest (when open). The hike between Manarola and Corniglia (#3) has minor hills (for a much steeper, more scenic alternative, consider detouring higher up, via Volastra—described later). The trail from Corniglia to Vernazza (#4) is demanding, and the path from Vernazza to Monterosso (#5) is the most challenging. Starting in Monterosso allows you to tackle the toughest section (with lots and lots of steep, narrow stairs) while you're fresh—and to enjoy some of the region's most dramatic scenery as you approach Vernazza. Remember that hikers need to pay a fee to enter the trails (see "Cinque Terre Park Cards," earlier).

Riomaggiore-Manarola (20 minutes): The popular, easy **Via dell'Amore** (as it's called) was washed out by a landslide in 2013;

the park hopes to reopen it by summer 2016—inquire locally. If it's open, facing the front of the train station in Riomaggiore (#1), go up the stairs to the right, following signs for *Via dell'Amore.* The photo-worthy promenade—wide enough for baby strollers—winds along the coast to Manarola (#2). While there's no beach along the trail, stairs lead down to sunbathing rocks. A long tunnel and mega-nets protect hikers from mean-spirited falling rocks. A recommended wine bar—Bar & Vini A Piè de Mà—is located at the Riomaggiore trailhead and offers light meals, awesome town views, and clever boat storage under the train tracks. There's a picnic zone with a water fountain, shade, and a seagull that must have been human in a previous life hanging out just above the Manarola station (WC at Manarola station). If the trail is closed, you can connect these towns by train...or, far more scenically, with a €4 boat trip.

Manarola-Corniglia (45 minutes): The walk from Manarola (#2) to Corniglia (#3, likely closed through mid-2016) is a little longer, more rugged, and steeper than the Via dell'Amore. It's also less romantic. To avoid the last stretch (switchback stairs leading up to the hill-capping town of Corniglia), end your hike at Corniglia's train station and catch the shuttle bus to the town center (2/hour, €1.50, free with Cinque Terre park card, usually timed to meet trains).

Corniglia-Vernazza (1.5 hours): The hike from Corniglia (#3) to Vernazza (#4)—the wildest and greenest section of the coast—is very rewarding but very hilly (going the other direction, from Vernazza to Corniglia, is steeper). From the Corniglia station and beach, zigzag up to the town (via the steep stairs, the longer road, or the shuttle bus). Keep going through vineyards toward Vernazza, and after about 10 minutes, you'll see Guvano beach far beneath you (once the region's nude beach). The scenic trail leads through lots of fragrant and flowery vegetation, into Vernazza. If

Via dell'Amore

The Cinque Terre towns were extremely isolated until the last century. Villagers rarely married anyone from outside their

town. After the blasting of a second train line in the 1920s, a trail was made between the first two towns, Riomaggiore and Manarola. The gunpowder warehouses built on each end, safely away from the townspeople, house cute little bars today.

Happy with the trail, the villagers asked that it be improved as a permanent connection between neighbors. But persistent landslides kept the trail closed more often than it was open. After World War II, the trail was reopened and became established as a lovers' meeting point for boys and girls from the two towns. (After one extended closure in 1949, the trail was reopened for a Christmas marriage.) A journalist who noticed all the amorous graffiti along the path coined the trail's now-established name, Via dell'Amore: "Pathway of Love."

This new lane changed the social dynamics between the two villages, and made life much more fun and interesting for courting couples. Today, many tourists are put off by the cluttered graffiti that lines the trail. But it's all part of the history of the Cinque Terre's little lovers' lane.

If the trail is open when you visit, you'll see padlocks locked to wires, cables, and fences. Closing a padlock with your lover at a lovey-dovey spot—often a bridge—is a common ritual in Italy (it was repopularized by a teen novel a few years ago). The hardware store next to Bar Centrale in Riomaggiore sells these locks. (You'll notice many of the locks come with the park logo.)

Major construction work has made the trail safer. Notice how the brick-lined arcades match the train tunnel below. Rock climbers from the north ("Dolomite spiders") were imported to help with the treacherous construction work. As you hike, look up and notice the massive steel netting bolted to the cliffside. Look down at the boulders that fell before the nets were added, and up at the boulders that have been caught... and be thankful for those Dolomite spiders.

Continuing the romance theme, benches along the way are named for lovers from Greek mythology. The many agave plants sport carved love notes—etched by amorous couples who likely don't know that the plant, which flowers once and then dies, is named for a tragic Greek story.

you need a break before reaching Vernazza, stop by Franco's Ristorante and Bar la Torre, with a strip of amazingly scenic and delightfully shady tables perched high above the town.

Vernazza-Monterosso (1.5 hours): The trail from Vernazza (#4) to Monterosso (#5) is a scenic up-and-down-a-lot trek and the most challenging of the bunch. Trails are narrow, steep, and crumbly, with a lot of steps (some readers report "very dangerous"), but easy to follow. Locals frown on camping at the picnic tables located midway. The views just out of Vernazza, looking back at the town, are spectacular. From there you'll gradually ascend, passing some scenic waterfalls populated by croaking frogs. As you approach Monterosso, you'll descend steeply—on very tall, knee-testing stairs—through vineyards, eventually following a rivulet to the sea. The last stretch into Monterosso is along a pleasant, paved pathway clinging to the cliff. You'll pop out right at Monterosso's refreshing old town beach.

Scenic Jogging: Very hardy joggers enjoy running between Monterosso and Vernazza (1.5 hours round-trip) or Vernazza and Corniglia (about an hour round-trip). But if you're not sure-footed, you may end up with a twisted ankle.

Longer Hikes

While the national park charges admission for the coastal trails, they also maintain a free, far more extensive network of trails higher in the hills. Shuttle buses make the going easier, connecting coastal villages and distant trailheads. For pointers, ask at a TI or park office—or anyone who's helpful (the Manarola-based Cinque Terre Trekking is a good resource).

Manarola-Volastra-Corniglia via the High Road (2.5 hours): One option—particularly if the Manarola-Corniglia trail is closed (and, if you're into serious hikes, even if it isn't)—is the hike from Manarola up to the village of Volastra, then north through high-altitude vineyard terraces, and steeply down through a forest to Corniglia (about six miles total). You can shave the two steepest miles off this route by taking the shuttle bus from Manarola up to Volastra (€1.50, free with Cinque Terre park card, schedule at park office, about hourly, 15 minutes). If you prefer to hike, you have two options for getting from Manarola to Volastra. The national park's official route (trail #6) cuts up through the valley, with less scenery. Locals have cleared a more scenic alternate route that begins with the vineyard hike on my self-guided walk for Manarola. Partway along this walk, when you reach the wooden religious scenes scampering up the hillside, take a sharp right and walk uphill, following the signs for *Volastra panoramica (Corniglia)*. While steeper than the official route, this trail follows the ridge at the top of the vineyard, providing wonderful sea views.

By shuttle bus or by one of the trails, you'll reach Volastra. This tiny village, perched between Manarola and Corniglia, hosts lots of Germans and Italians in the summer. (Just below its town center, in the hamlet of Groppo, is the Cinque Terre Cooperative Winery.) When you're ready to head for Corniglia, make your way to the village church (where the shuttle bus drops off) and look for *Corniglia* signs. You'll circle around to the front door of the church; directly across the piazza, find the trailhead (marked by an iron cross) for trail #6d to Case Pianca. Here begins one of the finest hikes in the region, tight-roping along narrow trails tucked between vineyard terraces, with spectacular bird's-eye views over the entire Cinque Terre. You'll cut up and down the terraces a bit—just keep following the red-and-white markings and arrows. After passing a little village (and following the signs through someone's seaview backyard), the trail enters a forest and begins its sharp, rocky descent into Corniglia. (To skip the descent, you could turn around and hike back through the vineyards to Volastra and return by shuttle bus to Manarola.) High above Corniglia, you'll reach a fork, where you turn left to proceed downhill on trail #7a to Corniglia.

Other Longer Hikes: If parts of the main coastal trail are closed and you're here for some serious hiking, get tips from locals on alternative trails. Popular options include **Vernazza to Reggio** (straight up the ridge, along Stations of the Cross, to the Sanctuary of Madonna; about an hour one-way, but easier if you take the shuttle bus from Vernazza); **Monterosso to Levanto** (about 3.5 hours one-way, moderately strenuous); and **Riomaggiore to Portovenere** (about 5 hours one-way; a challenging trek best for serious hikers). Be sure to get specific pointers before you set out.

Swimming, Kayaking, and Biking

Every town in the Cinque Terre has a beach or a rocky place to swim. Monterosso has the biggest and sandiest beach, with umbrellas and beach-use fees (but it's free where there are no umbrellas). Vernazza's main beach is tiny—better for sunning than swimming; the new, flood-created beach there is another option. Manarola, and Riomaggiore have the worst beaches (no sand), but Manarola offers the best deep-water swimming. Corniglia has no beach to speak of but does have sunning rocks.

Wear your walking shoes and pack your swim gear. Several of the beaches have showers (no shampoo, please). Underwater sightseeing is full of fish—goggles are sold in local shops. Sea urchins can be a problem if you walk on the rocks, and sometimes jellyfish wash up on the pebbles, so water shoes (or at least flip-flops) are essential.

You can rent kayaks or boats in Riomaggiore and Monterosso. (For details, see individual town listings in this chapter.) Some readers say kayaking can be dangerous—the kayaks tip easily, training is not provided, and lifejackets are not required.

SLEEPING IN THE CINQUE TERRE

If you think too many people have my book, avoid Vernazza. You get fewer crowds and better value for your money in other towns. Monterosso is a good choice for sun-worshipping softies, those who prefer the ease of a real hotel, and the younger crowd (more nightlife). Hermits, anarchists, wine lovers, and mountain goats like Corniglia. Sophisticated Italians and Germans choose charming but not overrun Manarola, which has a good range of (relatively) professional-feeling small accommodations, but limited dining options. Riomaggiore—bigger than Vernazza and less resorty than Monterosso—has the cheapest beds, but hoteliers there tend to be a bit flaky.

While the Cinque Terre is too rugged for the mobs that ravage the Spanish and French coasts, it's popular with Italians, Germans, and in-the-know Americans. Hotels charge more and are packed on holidays (including Easter); in May, June, and September; and on Fridays and Saturdays all summer. (With global warming, sweltering August is no longer considered peak season on this stretch of the Riviera.) While you can find doubles for about €70 most of the season, you'll pay extra in May and June. The prices I've listed are the maximum for April through October. For a terrace or view, you might pay an extra €20 or more. Apartments for four can be economical for families—figure around €120.

It's smart to reserve in advance in May, June, July, and September, and on weekends and holidays. At other times, you can

land a double room on any day just by arriving in town (ideally by noon) and asking around at bars and restaurants, or simply by approaching locals on the street. Many travelers enjoy the opportunity to shop around a bit and get the best price by bargaining. Private rooms—called *affitta camere*—are no longer an intimate stay with a family. They are generally comfortable apartments (often with small kitchens), where you get the key and come and go as you like, rarely seeing your landlord. Many landowners rent the buildings by the year to local managers, who then attempt to make a profit by filling them night after night with tourists. While air-conditioning is essential in the summer elsewhere in Italy, in the breezy Cinque Terre you can generally manage fine without it.

For the best value, visit several private rooms and snare the best deal. Going direct cuts out the middleman and softens prices. Staying more than one night gives you bargaining leverage. Plan on paying cash. Private rooms are generally bigger and more comfortable than those offered by pensions and have the same privacy as a hotel room.

Most private rooms don't include breakfast, so I've suggested alternatives in each town. The basic, very Italian choice is simply to drop by a neighborhood bar for a coffee and *cornetto* (croissant). Some pricier places "include breakfast," but this often consists of a few paltry items (yogurt, instant coffee, stale croissant) in a mini-fridge in your room.

If you want the security of a reservation, make it at a hotel long in advance (smaller places generally don't take reservations very far ahead). Reserve by email, and if you must cancel, do it as early as possible. Since people renting rooms usually don't take deposits, they lose money if you don't show up. The more formal places tend to have strict cancellation policies.

EATING IN THE CINQUE TERRE

Hanging out at a seaview restaurant while sampling local specialties could become one of your favorite memories.

The key staple here is anchovies (*acciughe;* ah-CHOO-gay)—ideally served the day they're caught. There's nothing cool about being an anchovy virgin. If you've always hated anchovies (the harsh, cured-in-salt American kind), try them fresh here. They can be prepared a variety of ways: marinated, salted, butterflied and deep-fried (sometimes with a delicious garlic/vinegar sauce called *giada*), and so on. *Tegame alla vernazzana* is the most typical main course in Vernazza: a layered, casserole-like dish of whole anchovies, potatoes, tomatoes, white wine, oil, and herbs.

While antipasto means cheese and salami in Tuscany, here you'll get *antipasti ai frutti di mare* (sometimes called simply *antipasti misti*), a plate of mixed "fruits of the sea" and a fine way to start a meal. Many restaurants are particularly proud of their *antipasti ai frutti di mare*—it's how they show off. For two diners, splitting one of these and a pasta dish can be plenty.

This region is the birthplace of pesto. Basil, which loves the temperate Ligurian climate, is ground with cheese (half parmigiano cow cheese and half pecorino sheep cheese), garlic, olive oil, and pine nuts, and then poured over pasta. Try it on spaghetti or, better yet, on *trenette* (the long, flat Ligurian noodle ruffled on one side) or *trofie* (short, dense twists made of flour with a bit of potato), both designed specifically for pesto to cling to. Many also like pesto lasagna, always made with white sauce, never red. If you become addicted, small jars of pesto are sold in the local grocery stores and gift shops. If it's refrigerated, it's fresh; this is what you want if you're eating it today. For taking home, get the jar-on-a-shelf pesto.

Pansotti are ravioli with ricotta and a mixture of greens, often served with a walnut sauce *(salsa di noci)*...delightful and filling.

Focaccia, the tasty pillowy bread, also originates here in Liguria. Locals say the best focaccia is made between the Cinque Terre and Genoa. It's simply flatbread with olive oil and salt. The baker roughs up the dough with finger holes, then bakes it. Focaccia comes plain or with onions, sage, or olive bits, and is a local favorite for a snack on the beach. Bakeries sell it in rounds or slices by weight (a portion is about 100 grams, or *un etto*).

Farinata, a humble flatbread snack sold at pizza and focaccia places, is made from chickpea meal, water, oil, and pepper and baked on a copper tray in a wood-burning stove.

The *vino delle Cinque Terre,* while not one of Italy's top wines, flows cheap and easy throughout the region. It's white—great with seafood. For a sweet dessert wine, the *Sciacchetrà* wine is worth the splurge (€4 per small glass, often served with dunkable cookies). You could order the fun dessert *torta della nonna* ("grandmother's cake") and dunk chunks of it into your glass. Aged *Sciacchetrà* is dry and costly (up to €12/glass). While 10 kilos of grapes yield 7 liters of local wine, *Sciacchetrà* is made from near-raisins, and 10 kilos of grapes make only 1.5 liters of *Sciacchetrà.* The word means "push and pull"—push in lots of grapes, pull out the best wine. If your room is up a lot of steps, be warned: *Sciacchetrà* is 18 percent alcohol, while regular wine is only 11 percent.

In the cool, calm evening, sit on Vernazza's breakwater with a glass of wine and watch the phosphorescence in the waves.

NIGHTLIFE IN THE CINQUE TERRE

While the Cinque Terre is certainly not noted for bumping beach-town nightlife like nearby Viareggio, you'll find some sort of travel-tale-telling hub in Monterosso, Vernazza, and Riomaggiore (Manarola and Corniglia are sleepy). Monterosso (where bars can stay open until 2:00 in the morning) has a lively scene, especially in the summertime—but no *discoteca*...yet. In Vernazza, the nightlife centers in the bars on the waterfront piazza, which is the small-town-style place to "see and be seen." A town law requires all bars to shut by midnight. In Riomaggiore, Bar Centrale is the, well, central place for cocktails and meeting fellow travelers. (For details, see the "Nightlife" sections for these three villages.) Wherever your night adventures take you, have fun, but please remember that residents live upstairs.

HELPFUL HINTS FOR THE CINQUE TERRE

Tourist and Park Information: Each town has a well-staffed park information office, which generally serves as an all-purpose town TI as well (listed throughout this chapter).

Money: Banks and ATMs are plentiful throughout the region.

Internet Access: All Cinque Terre train stations offer free Wi-Fi with a Cinque Terre park card.

Baggage Storage: You can store bags at La Spezia's train station (€3/12 hours, daily 8:00-22:00), at the gift shop in Vernazza's train station (€1/hour for the first 5 hours, daily 8:00-20:00, closed Nov-March), and at the Wash and Dry Lavarapido in Monterosso (€5/day).

Services: Every train station has a free WC, but it's smart to bring your own toilet paper. Otherwise, pop into a bar or restaurant.

Taxi: Cinqueterre Taxi covers all five towns (mobile 334-776-1946 or 347-652-0837, www.cinqueterretaxi.com).

Booking Agency: Miriana at **Cinque Terre Riviera** books rooms in the Cinque Terre towns, Portovenere, and La Spezia for a 10 percent markup over the list price (ask about discounts for properties they manage; can also arrange transportation, cooking classes, and weddings; Via Roma 24 in Vernazza, tel. 0187-812-123, mobile 340-794-7358, www.cinqueterreriviera.com, info@cinqueterreriviera.com, English spoken).

Local Guides: Andrea Bordigoni is both knowledgeable and a delight (€110/half-day, €175/day, mobile 393-133-9409, bordigo@inwind.it). Other local guides are **Marco Brizzi** (mobile 328-694-2847, www.hi-ke.com, marco_brizzi@yahoo.it) and **Paola Tommarchi** (paolatomma@alice.it).

Tours and Activities: ArbaSPàa, which has an office in Manarola, can arrange Cinque Terre experiences that might be tricky to do on your own, such as wine tasting at a vineyard, cooking classes (6-person minimum), or a fishing trip with local sailors (see website for options and book in advance, tel. 0187-920-783, www.arbaspaa.com; their Explora shop in Manarola, at Via Discovolo 252/A, is closed Tue).

Tour Packages for Students: Andy Steves (Rick's son) runs **Weekend Student Adventures** (WSA Europe), offering three-day and longer guided and unguided packages—including accommodations, sightseeing, and unique local experiences—for student travelers in the Cinque Terre and top European cities (guided trips from €199, see www.wsaeurope.com).

Useful Blog: Anna Merulla runs the **BeautifuLiguria** blog, where she shares cultural and offbeat insights into the region and organizes excursions and tours (www.beautifuliguria.com).

Riomaggiore (Town #1)

The most substantial non-resort town of the group, Riomaggiore is a disappointment from the train station. But just walk through the tunnel next to the train tracks, and you'll discover a more real, laid-back, and workaday town than its touristy neighbors. The main drag through town, while traffic-free, feels more urban than "village," and surrounding the harbor is a fascinating tangle of pastel homes leaning on each other like drunken sailors.

Orientation to Riomaggiore

TOURIST INFORMATION

The TI is in the train station at the ticket desk (daily 8:00-20:00, shorter hours off-season, tel. 0187-920-633). If the TI in the station is crowded, buy your hiking pass at the Cinque Terre park shop/information office next door, facing the mural (same hours as TI, tel. 0187-760-515). For informal information sources, try Ivo and Alberto, who run the recommended Bar Centrale or Amy and Francesco, who run Riomaggiore Reservations (see "Sleeping in Riomaggiore," later).

ARRIVAL IN RIOMAGGIORE

By Train: Riomaggiore's train station is separated from the town center by a steep hill (which you can summit for fine views by following my self-guided walk). The easiest way to get into town is to take the pedestrian tunnel that begins by the big mural (and parallels the rail tunnel). You'll exit at the bottom of Via Colombo; most recommended hotels are a short hike up this steep artery. If you're staying near the top of town, you can catch the shuttle bus (described next) at the bottom of Via Colombo and ride it partway up, or ride the elevator up from the pedestrian tunnel (€1/person, daily 7:00-18:00).

By Car: Day-trippers park at one of two pay-and-display lots above town (€3.50/hour, €23/day, best to pay in cash). If staying overnight, your hotel may have parking. Otherwise, Riomaggiore allows overnighters to drive into the town center long enough to drop off or pick up bags, but only during designated times (confirm with your hotelier).

HELPFUL HINTS

Internet Access: The **park shop/information office** has four public computers with Internet access upstairs, plus Wi-Fi (€1.50/20 minutes, free with Cinque Terre park card, daily 8:00-20:00, shorter hours off-season). The recommended **La Zorza Café** and **Bar Centrale** both offer free Wi-Fi with the purchase of a drink.

Services: There's a WC near the Co-op grocery on Via Colombo, and another under the tunnel where the street dead-ends.

Laundry: A self-service launderette is on the main street (daily in summer 8:30-20:00, shorter hours off-season, Via Colombo 107).

Riomaggiore Walk

Here's a partly uphill but easy self-guided loop walk that takes the long way around from the station into town. You'll enjoy some fine views before strolling down the main street to the harbor.

• *Start at the train station. (If you arrive by boat, cross beneath the tracks and take a left, then hike through the tunnel along the tracks to reach the station.) You'll see some...*

Colorful Murals: These murals, with subjects modeled after real-life Riomaggiorians, glorify the nameless workers who con-

structed the nearly 300 million cubic feet of dry-stone walls (made without mortar) that run throughout the Cinque Terre. These walls give the region its characteristic *muri a secco* terracing for vineyards and olive groves. The murals, created by Argentinean artist Silvio Benedetto, are explained well in English.

Looking left, notice the stairs climbing up just past the station building. These lead to the trail to Manarola, also known as the **Via dell'Amore**.

• *The fastest way into town is to take the pedestrian tunnel (which parallels the tracks from near the murals) straight to the bottom of Via Colombo, just above the marina. But I'd rather take the scenic route, up and over the hill. Facing the mural, turn left, then go right up the wide street just before the station café. Watch for the stairs leading through the garden on your right to the upper switchback, then, once on high ground, hook back toward the sea. Soon you'll pass the concrete tower marking the top of an elevator near the tunnel entrance, and a bit farther, a fine viewpoint.*

Top o' the Town: Here you're treated to spectacular sea views.

Hook left around the bluff; once you round the bend, ignore the steps marked *Marina Seacoast* (which lead to the harbor) and continue another five minutes along level ground to the church. You'll pass under the city hall, with murals celebrating the heroic grape-pickers and fishermen of the region (also by Silvio Benedetto).

• *Before reaching the church, pause to enjoy the...*

Town View: The major river of this region once ran through this valley, as implied by the name Riomaggiore (local dialect for "river" and "major"). As in the other Cinque Terre towns, the river ravine is now paved over, and the romantic arched bridges that once connected the two sides have been replaced by a practical modern road.

Notice the lack of ugly aerial antennae. In the 1980s, every residence got cable. Now, the TV tower on the hilltop behind the church steeple brings the modern world into each home. The church was rebuilt in 1870, but was first established in 1340. It's dedicated to St. John the Baptist, the patron saint of Genoa, the maritime republic that once dominated the region.

• *Continue straight past the church and along the narrow lane, watching on the right for wide stairs leading down to Riomaggiore's main street...*

Via Colombo: As in the other Cinque Terre towns, the main street of Riomaggiore covers its *rio maggiore,* which carved the canyon now filled by the town's pastel high-rises. Then start downhill. First you'll pass (on the right, at #62) a good pizzeria/*focacceria,* facing the Co-op grocery store across the street (at #55). Farther down on the left is the town butcher (*macelleria,* #103). The big covered terrace on the right belongs to Bar Centrale, the town's most popular hangout for international visitors (at #144; see "Nightlife in Riomaggiore," later). Just after the terrace sits a forlorn row of recycling containers, with careful instructions that are ignored by locals and tourists alike.

As you round the bend to the left, notice the old-timey pharmacy just above (on the right). On your left, at #199, peek into the Il Pescato Cucinato shop, where Laura fries up her husband Edoardo's fresh catch; grab a paper cone of deep-fried seafood as a snack. Where the road bends sharply right, notice the bench on your left (just before La Zorza Café)—the hangout for the town's old-timers, who keep a running commentary on the steady flow of people. Straight ahead, you can already see where this street will dead-end. The last shop on the left, Alimentari Franca (at #251), is a well-stocked grocery where you can gather the makings for a perfect picnic out on the harbor or along the Via dell'Amore.

Where Via Colombo dead-ends, look right to see the tunnel leading back to the station (and the Via dell'Amore to Manarola, and eventually to the other Cinque Terre towns). Look left to see two sets of stairs. The "up" stairs take you to a park-like square built over the train tracks, which provides the children of the town a bit of level land on which to kick their soccer balls. The murals above celebrate the great-grandparents of these very children—the salt-of-the-earth locals who earned a humble living before the age of tourism.

• *The "down" stairs take you to a pay WC and the...*

Marina: This most picturesque corner of Riomaggiore features a tight cluster of buildings huddling nervously around a postage-stamp square and vest-pocket harbor. Because Riomaggiore lacks the naturally protected harbor of Vernazza, when bad weather is expected, local fishermen pull their boats up to the safety of the little square. This is quite an operation, so it's a team effort—the signal goes out, and anyone with a boat of their own helps move the whole fleet. Sometimes the fishermen are busy beaching their boats even on a bright, sunny day—an indication that they know something you don't know.

A couple of recommended restaurants—with high prices and memorable seating—look down over the action. Head past them and up the walkway along the left side of the harbor, and enjoy the views of the town's colorful pastel buildings, with the craggy coastline of the Cinque Terre just beyond. Below you, the break-water curves out to sea, providing a bit of protection for the harbor. These rocks are popular with sunbathers by day and romantics and photographers at sunset.

For a peek at Riomaggiore's beach, continue around the bluff on this trail toward the Punta di Montenero, the cape that defines the southern end of the Cinque Terre. As you walk you'll pass the rugged boat landing and eventually run into Riomaggiore's un-comfortably rocky but still inviting beach *(spiaggia)*. Ponder how Europeans manage to look relaxed when lounging on football-sized "pebbles."

Experiences in Riomaggiore

Beach

Riomaggiore's rugged and tiny "beach" is rocky, but it's clean and peaceful (to find it, see the end of my self-guided walk, above). There's a shower here in the summer, and another closer to town by the boat landing—where many enjoy sunning on and jumping from the rocks.

Kayaks and Water Sports

The town has a diving center (scuba, snorkeling, kayaks; office down the stairs and under the tracks on Via San Giacomo, daily May-Sept 9:00-18:00, open in good weather only—likely weekends only in shoulder season, tel. 0187-920-011, www.5terrediving.it).

To Manarola

♥ Via dell'Amore ♥

Cliffs

Ligurian Sea

PARK OFFICE KIOSK
TRAIN STATION

WALK BEGINS

MURALS

CINQUE TERRE INFO

ELEVATOR TO TOP OF TOWN (INSIDE PED. TUNNEL)

VIA PECUNIA

VIA SIGNORINI

PEDESTRIAN TUNNEL →

VIA SANT'ANTONIO

PUNTA VIA

Piazza Vignaioli

WC (UNDER TUNNEL)

Cliffs

BOAT DOCK

Harbor

VIA SAN GIACOMO

BREAKWATER

BOAT TICKETS

① Riomaggiore Reservations (Office), Il Pescato Cucinato, Giammi Caffè & Co-op Grocery

② Edi's Rooms & Launderette

③ L'Ancora Rooms

④ Alla Marina Rooms; Enoteca & Ristorante Dau Cila

⑤ La Dolce Vita Rooms

⑥ Il BoMa Rooms

⑦ Hotel del Sole

⑧ Locanda dalla Compagnia

⑨ Camere Patrizia

⑩ Trattoria la Grotta & Il Grottino Ristorante

⑪ Bar Centrale & Gelateria

⑫ Pizzeria/Focacceria

⑬ Siamo Fritti

⑭ Alimentari Franca

⑮ Bar & Vini A Piè de Mà

⑯ La Zorza Café

⑰ Co-op Grocery

Hikes

It's possible to hike from here all the way to Portovenere (about 5 strenuous hours). Some easier alternatives are also available. A trail rises scenically from Riomaggiore to the 14th-century Madonna di Montenero sanctuary, high above the town (45 minutes, take the main road inland until you see signs, or ride the shuttle bus 12 minutes from the town center to the sanctuary trail, then walk up-hill another 10 minutes; great picnic spot up top). The cliff-hanging Torre Guardiola trail, a steep 20-minute climb from the beach up to old WWII bunkers and a hilltop botanical pathway, is closed indefinitely.

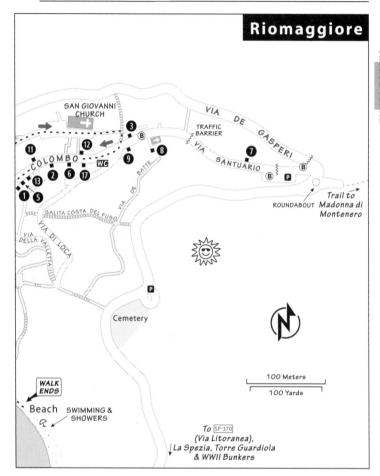

Riomaggiore

SAN GIOVANNI CHURCH

VIA DE GASPERI

TRAFFIC BARRIER

VIA SANTUARIO

COLOMBO

VIA DE BATTE

Trail to Madonna di Montenero

ROUNDABOUT

SALITA COSTA DEL FUSO

VIA DELLA VALLETTA

VIA DI LOCA

Cemetery

100 Meters

100 Yards

WALK ENDS

Beach SWIMMING & SHOWERS

To SP-370 (Via Litoranea), La Spezia, Torre Guardiola & WWII Bunkers

Nightlife in Riomaggiore

Bar Centrale, run by sociable Ivo, Alberto, and the gang, offers "nightlife" any time of day—making it a good stop for Italian breakfast and music. Ivo, who lived in San Francisco, fills his bar with San Franciscan rock and a fun-loving vibe. During the day, this is a shaded place to relax with other travelers; it feels a little like the village's living room. At night, it offers the younger set the liveliest action (and best mojitos) in town (daily 7:30-1:00 in the morning, closed Mon in winter, 30 minutes of free Wi-Fi with drink, in the town center at Via Colombo 144, tel. 0187-920-208). They also serve pasta, pizza, and American comfort food until late, and gelato next door.

Enoteca & Ristorante Dau Cila, a cool little hideaway with a mellow jazz-and-Brazilian-lounge ambience down at the minuscule harbor, is a counterpoint to wild Bar Centrale. It's cool for cocktails and open nightly until 24:00 (snacks and meals, fine wine by the glass; see "Eating in Riomaggiore," later).

Bar & Vini A Piè de Mà, at the beginning of Via dell'Amore, has piles of charm, €6 cocktails, frequent music, and stays open until midnight June through September (see "Eating in Riomaggiore," later).

La Zorza Café is a hip, youthful alternative to the other bars in town. The music is thumping, and the cocktails, prepared by a free-style bartender, come with a spread of little snacks (€6 cocktails, spring-fall daily until late, winter until 21:00, free Wi-Fi with drink, tel. 0187-920-036, fun-loving Elenia).

The marvelous **Via dell'Amore** trail, lit only with subtle ground lighting so that you can see the stars, welcomes romantics after dark. When open, the trail is free after 19:30.

Sleeping in Riomaggiore

Riomaggiore has arranged its private-room rental system somewhat better than its neighbors. Several agencies—with relatively predictable office hours, English-speaking staff, and email addresses—line up within a few yards of each other on the main drag. Each manages a corral of local rooms for rent—but be aware that quality and specific amenities can vary wildly, so get a complete picture of the room before you commit. These offices sometimes close unexpectedly, so it's smart to settle up the day before you leave in case they're closed when you need to depart. Expect lots of stairs.

ROOM-BOOKING SERVICES

Given the relatively lousy value of Riomaggiore's hotels (see next section), I'd contact one of these services first. Very few of these rooms include breakfast.

$$ Riomaggiore Reservations, run with care and smooth communication by American expat Amy and her Italian husband Francesco, offers seven rooms and six apartments (Db-€70-100 depending on view, Db suite with top view-€130, cash only, discount with this book in 2016, reception open daily 9:00-13:00 & 14:00-17:00 in season, some rooms have air-con, Via Colombo 181, tel. 0187-760-575, www.riomaggiorereservations.com, info@riomaggiorereservations.com).

$$ Edi's Rooms manages one double room and 12 apartments. You pay extra for views (Db-€70-80, apartment Qb-€140-180, office open daily in summer 8:30-20:00, in winter 10:30-12:30 & 14:30-18:00, some apartments involve climbing a lot of steps—ask, some have air-con, closed Jan-Feb, reception at Via

---

Sleep Code

Abbreviations   **(€1=about $1.10, country code: 39)**
S=Single, **D**=Double/Twin, **T**=Triple, **Q**=Quad, **b**=bathroom
Price Rankings
  $$$ Higher Priced—Most rooms €100 or more
   $$ Moderately Priced—Most rooms €50-100
    $ Lower Priced—Most rooms €50 or less
Unless otherwise noted, credit cards are accepted, free Wi-Fi and/or a guest computer is generally available, English is spoken, and breakfast is included (except in some private rooms and in Vernazza). Many towns in Italy levy a hotel tax of €1.50-5 per person, per night (often collected in cash; usually not included in the rates I've quoted). Prices change; verify current rates online or by email. For the best prices, always book directly with the hotel.

Colombo 111, tel. 0187-760-842, www.appartamenticinqueterre. net, edi-vesigna@iol.it). They also rent three hotelesque but pricey rooms of their own, called **L'Ancora** (Db-€120, air-con, www. lancoracinqueterre.com).

PRIVATE ROOMS

Another option is to book direct with someone who rents just a few rooms of their own, cutting out the middleman. Here are some options.

$$$ Alla Marina is Riomaggiore's most worthwhile splurge, with three rooms and an apartment at the top of one of the very tall, steep, skinny buildings that rise up from the harbor. The furnishings are a stylish combination of modern and nautical, and friendly brothers Sandro and Andrea take pride in running a tight ship (non-view Db-€100; all others with sea views: Db-€130, Tb-€140, Qb-€190; 10 percent discount with this book in 2016, includes in-room breakfast, snacks, air-con, free minibar, parking-€10/day; Via San Giacomo 61—ask about the easier back-door entrance; mobile 328-013-4077, www.allamarina.com, info@ allamarina.com).

$$ La Dolce Vita offers six nice, good-value rooms on the main drag, plus two apartments elsewhere in town (Db-€70-85, open daily 9:30-19:30—if they're closed, they're full; Via Colombo 167, tel. 0187-762-283, agonatal@libero.it, helpful Giacomo and Simone).

$$ Il BoMa—named for the owners, American Maddy and her Italian husband Bombetta—has three pricey but well-appointed rooms right along the main drag. They also rent two nearby apartments—email for details (Db-€90, includes in-room breakfast with freshly baked brioche, one room has private bathroom down the hall and fans, others have air-con, up three flights at Via Colombo 99, tel. 0187-920-395, mobile 320-0748826, www.ilboma.com, info@ilboma.it).

HOTELS
Perhaps sensing that they have little "hotel" competition, these generally offer less value than room-booking services and private rooms. Breakfast is included.

$$$ Hotel del Sole has seven modern, basic, and overpriced rooms with a shared and peaceful terrace. Located at the utilitarian top end of town, it's a five-minute walk downhill to the center. Easy (and free with this book in 2016) parking makes it especially appealing to drivers (Db-€130, extra bed-€20, ask for Rick Steves discount when you book directly with hotel and pay cash, air-con, Via Santuario 114, tel. 0187-920-773, mobile 340-983-0090, www.locandadelsole.net, info@locandadelsole.net, Enrico).

$$ Locanda dalla Compagnia, loosely run by Alessandro, rents five rooms at the top of town, just 300 yards below the parking lot and the little church. All rooms—decent but rather dim—are on the same tranquil ground floor and share a lounge (Db-€80, air-con, mini-fridge, no views, reception closes at 19:00, Via del Santuario 232, tel. 0187-760-050, www.dallacompa.com, lacomp@libero.it). Alessandro also manages nine apartments scattered around town (€10 more than his hotel rooms, no breakfast).

BACKPACKER DORM
$ Camere Patrizia, a suitable last resort, rents cheap doubles (Db-€60, €70 on weekends) and dorm bunk beds (€25/person) from its reception at Via Colombo 25, but books only through www.hostelworld.com or to drop-ins (reception open daily 10:30-20:00, mobile 328-309-3727 or 366-298-3113).

Eating in Riomaggiore

ON THE HARBOR
Harborfront dining comes with slightly higher prices but glorious views.

Enoteca & Ristorante Dau Cila (pronounced "dow CHEE-lah") is decked out like a black-and-white movie set in a centuries-old boat shed with extra tables outside on a rustic deck over dinghies. Try their antipasto specialty of several seafood appetizers and listen to the waves lapping at the harbor below (€12-19 pastas, €15-18 *secondi;* for lunch, they also have a simpler menu—€9-12 salads and *bruschette;* daily 12:00-24:00, closed Jan-Feb and Mon in March, Via San Giacomo 65, tel. 0187-760-032, Luca).

ON THE MAIN STREET, VIA COLOMBO

Trattoria la Grotta, right in the town center (with no view), serves reliably good food with a passion for anchovies and mussels. You'll enjoy friendly service surrounded by historical photos and wonderful stonework in a dramatic, dressy, cave-like setting. Vanessa is warm and helpful, while her mother, Isa, is busy cooking (€11-14 pastas, €11-15 *secondi,* daily 12:00-14:30 & 17:30-22:30, closed Thu in winter, Via Colombo 247, tel. 0187-920-187). Next door and run by the same family, **Il Grottino Ristorante** is slightly more upscale, with a similar approach and decor and a somewhat different menu (same hours, tel. 0187-920-938). I'd survey both to see which specials look good.

Bar Centrale, the popular bar and expat hangout, serves €8-10 pizza, pasta, and popular American fare; drop by to scope out their menu (see "Nightlife in Riomaggiore," earlier).

Light Meals: Various handy carry-out eateries along the main drag offer good lunches or snacks. At the top of town, the nameless **pizzeria/focacceria** at #62 is a reliable standby (€3 slices). For deep-fried seafood in a paper cone, two places face each other across the main street near the bottom of town; of these, I prefer **Il Pescato Cucinato,** where Edoardo fishes and his wife Laura fries (€5-9, chalkboard out front explains what's fresh, daily 11:20-20:30, Via Colombo 199, mobile 339-262-4815). A few doors away, **Siamo Fritti** has €5-9 fried fish (daily 10:00-21:00, Via Colombo 161, mobile 347-826-1729, Andrea and Isabella).

Picnics: Groceries and delis lining Via Colombo sell food to go for a picnic at the harbor or beach. Look for the two **Co-op** grocery store signs for the best prices. The handy **Alimentari Franca,** at the very bottom of the main street (conveniently located right by the train-station tunnel and stairs down to the marina/beach) has a more appealing selection and good service (Thu-Tue 8:00-12:45 & 15:30-19:00, closed Wed in winter, Via Colombo 251).

Breakfast: While hotels include breakfast, many private rooms don't, and those that do often simply leave a coffee kettle and some basic continental breakfast fixings in your room. If you need eggs or a good croissant-and-espresso fix, drop by **Bar Centrale** (€6 egg dishes). Or, consider **Giammi Caffè,** with outdoor tables on the main drag (€6 egg dishes, €13 big breakfast, daily 7:00-24:00, Via Colombo 189, mobile 331-608-3512).

NEAR THE TRAIN STATION AND VIA DELL'AMORE

Bar & Vini A Piè de Mà, at the trailhead on the Manarola end of town, is good for a scenic light bite or quiet drink at night. The downstairs bar, with great outdoor seating, is self-service: Head into the bar to place your order, then bring it out to your preferred perch (€8-12 dishes, €4 *panini,* daily 10:00-20:00, June-Sept until

24:00, free Wi-Fi—look for password on chalkboard, tel. 0187-921-037). Enjoying a meal at a table on its dramatically situated terrace provides an indelible Cinque Terre memory. In the summer they open a restaurant with table service upstairs—but I prefer the cheaper, simpler terrace.

Manarola (Town #2)

Mellow Manarola fills a ravine, bookended by its wild little harbor to the west and a diminutive hilltop church square inland to the east. Manarola is exceptional for being unexceptional: While Vernazza is prettier, Monterosso glitzier, Riomaggiore bigger, and Corniglia more rustic, each of those towns is also sorely lacking in other regards. Manarola hits a fine balance, giving it the "just right" combination of Cinque Terre qualities. Perhaps that's why it's a favorite among savvy Europeans seeking a relatively untrampled home base. The touristy zone squeezed between the cement-encased train tracks and the harbor can be stressfully congested, but head just a few steps uphill and you can breathe again. The higher you go, the less crowded it gets, culminating in the essentially tourist-free residential zone that clings to the ridge.

Manarola, whose hillsides are blanketed with vineyards, also provides the easiest access to the Cinque Terre's remarkable dry-stone terraces. The trail ringing the town's cemetery peninsula, adjacent to the main harbor, provides some of the most easily accessible and most strikingly beautiful town views anywhere in the region (best light late in the day). For a look at all the facets of this delightful town, follow my gentle self-guided stroll from the church, through the vineyards, and down to the harborside park.

Orientation to Manarola

Tourist Information: The TI/national park information office is in the train station (likely daily 7:30-19:30, shorter hours off-season).

Getting Around: The ATC **shuttle bus** runs from near the post office (halfway up Manarola's main street), stopping first at the parking lots above town, and then going all the way up to Volastra (€1.50 one-way, buy ticket on board for €2.50, free with Cinque Terre park card, about hourly). Volastra is a great jumping-off point for a scenic hike through vineyards and forests to

Corniglia (more challenging—and rewarding—than the official coastal trail).

To get to the **dock** and the boats that connect Manarola with the other Cinque Terre towns, find the steps to the left of the harbor view—they lead down to the ticket kiosk. Continue around the left side of the cliff (as you're facing the water) to catch the boats.

Hiking Gear and Tips: Cinque Terre Trekking, near the top of the main street (halfway up to the church), fills its cramped little shop with hiking gear (boots, clothes, walking sticks, and more); they also sell hiking maps and offer free advice (daily 9:00-13:00 & 14:00-20:00, shorter hours off-season, Via Discovolo 136, tel. 0187-920-715).

ARRIVAL IN MANAROLA

On Foot: Walking in from Riomaggiore on the Via dell'Amore, you'll pop out at Manarola's train station (see next).

By Train: Like Riomaggiore, Manarola is attached to its station by a 200-yard-long tunnel (lined with interesting photos). During WWII air raids, these tunnels provided refuge and a safe place for rattled villagers to sleep. Walking through the tunnel, you'll reach Manarola's elevated square (created by covering the tracks). To reach the busy harbor (with touristy restaurants, the boat dock, and the start of my self-guided walk), cross the piazza, then go down the other side. To reach the town, hilltop church, and vineyard strolls, turn right.

By Car: Unless you're sleeping here, you're not allowed to drive into Manarola. Park your car in one of the two lots just before town (€2/hour), then walk down the road to the church; from there, the street twists down to the main piazza, train-station tunnel (to reach the trailhead for the Via dell'Amore to Riomaggiore), and harbor (the start of my self-guided walk). It's an easy downhill walk into town, or you can wait for the shuttle bus (described earlier). If you're sleeping here, ask your hotelier for parking advice.

Manarola Walk

From the harbor, this 30-minute self-guided circular walk shows you the town and surrounding vineyards and ends at a fantastic viewpoint, perfect for a picnic.

• *Start down at the waterfront. Belly up to the wooden banister overlooking the rocky harbor, between the two restaurants.*

The Harbor: Manarola is tiny and picturesque, a tumble of buildings bunny-hopping down its ravine to the

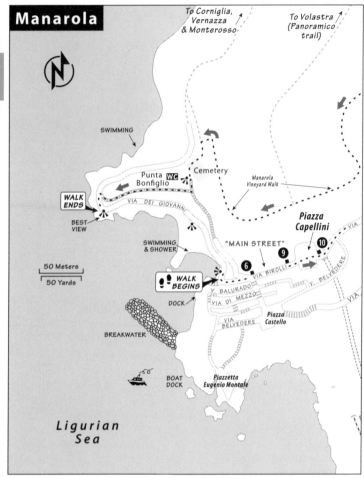

fun-loving waterfront. The breakwater—which attempts to make this jagged harbor a bit less dangerous—was built just over a decade ago. Notice how the I-beam crane launches the boats (which must be pulled ashore when bad weather is expected to avoid being smashed or swept away).

Facing the water, look up to the right, at the hillside Punta Bonfiglio cemetery and park. The trail running around the base of the point—where this walk ends—offers magnificent views back on this part of town.

The town's swimming hole is just below you. Manarola has no sand, but offers the best deep-water swimming in the area. The first "beach" has a shower, ladder, and wonderful rocks. The second has tougher access and no shower, but feels more remote and pristine

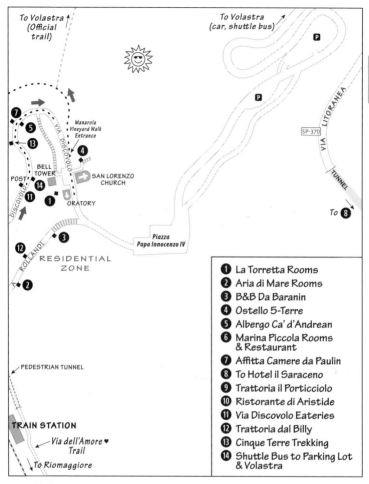

To Volastra ↑
(Official
trail)

To Volastra
(car, shuttle bus)

P

P

P

VIA DISCOVOLO

VIA LITORANEA

SP-370

TUNNEL

Manarola
Vineyard Walk
Entrance

❼

❺

❿ ⓭

❹

BELL
TOWER

SAN LORENZO
CHURCH

POST

⓮

❶

❾

ORATORY

DISCOVOLO

❿ ❶

To ❽

❸

ROLLANDI

Piazza
Papa Innocenzo IV

⓬

RESIDENTIAL
ZONE

❷

PEDESTRIAN TUNNEL

TRAIN STATION

Via dell'Amore ♥
Trail

To Riomaggiore

❶ La Torretta Rooms
❷ Aria di Mare Rooms
❸ B&B Da Baranin
❹ Ostello 5-Terre
❺ Albergo Ca' d'Andrean
❻ Marina Piccola Rooms
  & Restaurant
❼ Affitta Camere da Paulin
❽ To Hotel il Saraceno
❾ Trattoria il Porticciolo
❿ Ristorante di Aristide
⓫ Via Discovolo Eateries
⓬ Trattoria dal Billy
⓭ Cinque Terre Trekking
⓮ Shuttle Bus to Parking Lot
  & Volastra

(follow the paved path toward Corniglia, just around the point). For many, the tricky access makes this "beach" dangerous.

• *Hiking inland up the town's main drag—comparison-shopping at the touristy restaurants—you'll climb a steep ramp to reach Manarola's "new" square, which covers the train tracks.*

Piazza Capellini: Built in 2004, this square is an all-around great idea, giving the town a safe, fun zone for kids. Locals living near the tracks also enjoy a little less train noise. Check out the mosaic in the middle of the square, which depicts the varieties of local fish in colorful enamel. The recommended Ristorante di Aristide has an inviting terrace right out on the square.

• *Go down the stairs at the upper end of the square. On your right, notice the tunnel that leads to Manarola's train station (and the trailhead for the Via dell'Amore to Riomaggiore). But for now, head up...*

Via Discovolo: Manarola's sleepy main street twists up through town, lined by modest shops and filled with pooped hikers. Just before the road bends sharply right, watch (on the right) for a waterwheel. This recalls the origin of the town's name—local dialect for "big wheel" (one of many possible derivations). Mills like this once powered the local olive oil industry. As you continue up (all the way to the church), you'll still hear the rushing waters of Manarola's stream. Like the streams in Riomaggiore, Monterosso, and Vernazza, Manarola's rivulet was covered over by a modern sewage system after World War II. Before that time, romantic bridges arched over its ravine. You can peek below the concrete street in several places to see the stream surging below your feet.

Across the street from the waterwheel and a bit farther up, notice the **Cinque Terre Trekking** shop (on your left), which outfits hikers with both information and gear.

• *Keep switchbacking up until you come to the square at the...*

Top of Manarola: The square is faced by a church, an oratory—now a religious and community meeting place—and a bell tower, which served as a watchtower when pirates raided the town (the cupola was added once the attacks ceased). Behind the church is Manarola's well-run youth hostel, originally the church's schoolhouse. To the right of the oratory, a stepped lane leads to Manarola's sizable tourist-free residential zone.

Check out the **church.** According to the white marble plaque in its facade, the Parish Church of St. Lawrence (San Lorenzo) dates from "MCCCXXXVIII" (1338). Step inside to see two altarpiece paintings from the unnamed Master of the Cinque Terre, the only painter of any note from this region (left wall and above main altar). While the style is Gothic, the work dates from the late 15th century, long after Florence had entered the Renaissance. Note the humble painted stone ceiling, which replaced the wooden original in the 1800s. It features Lawrence, patron saint of the Cinque Terre, with his grill, the symbol of his martyrdom (he was roasted on it).

• *With the bell tower on your left, head about 20 yards down the main street below the church and find a wooden railing. It marks the start of a delightful stroll around the high side of town, and back to the seafront. This is the beginning of the...*

Manarola Vineyard Walk: Don't miss this experience. Simply follow the wooden railing, enjoying lemon groves and wild red valerian (used for insomnia since the days of the Romans). Along the path, which is primarily flat, you'll get a close-up look at the region's famous dry-stone walls and finely crafted vineyards (with dried-heather thatches to protect the grapes from the southwest winds). Smell the rosemary. Study the structure of the town, and pick out the scant remains of an old fort. Notice the S-shape of the main road—once a riverbed—that flows through town. The town's roofs are traditionally made of locally quarried slate, rather than tile, and are held down by rocks during windstorms.

Halfway along the lip of the ravine, a path marked *Volastra panoramico (Corniglia)* leads steeply up into the vineyards on the right. This path passes a variety of simple wooden religious scenes, the work of local resident Mario Andreoli. Before his father died, Mario promised him he'd replace the old cross on the family's vineyard. Mario has been adding figures ever since. After recovering from a rare illness, he redoubled his efforts. On religious holidays, everything's lit up: the Nativity, the Last Supper, the Crucifixion, the Resurrection, and more. Some of the scenes are left up year-round. High above, a recent fire burned off the tree cover, revealing ancient terraces that line the terrain like a topographic map. This path also marks the start of the scenic route to Volastra (on the hilltop above), and eventually to Corniglia.

• *Continue on the level trail around the base of the hill. Soon the harbor comes into view. Keep looping around the hill for even better views of town. Once you're facing the sea (with the cemetery peninsula below you), the trail takes a sharp left and heads down toward the water. When you hit the clifftop fence, the T-intersection gives you a choice: right, to the coastal trail to Corniglia, or left, back to town. Turn left for now. Before descending, watch for the turnoff on the right, detouring into...*

The Cemetery: Ever since Napoleon—who was king of Italy in the early 1800s—decreed that cemeteries were health risks, Cinque Terre's burial spots have been located outside the towns. The result: The dearly departed generally get first-class sea views. Each cemetery—with evocative yellowed photos and finely carved Carrara marble memorial reliefs—is worth a visit. (The basic structure for all of them is the same, but Manarola's is the most easily accessible.)

In cemeteries like these, there's a hierarchy of four places to park your mortal remains: a graveyard, a spacious death condo *(loculo)*, a mini bone-niche *(ossario)*, or the communal ossuary. Because of the tight space, a time limit is assigned to the first three options (although many older tombs are grandfathered in). Bones go into the ossuary in the middle of the chapel floor after about a generation. Traditionally, locals make weekly visits to loved ones here, often bringing flowers. The rolling stepladder makes access to top-floor *loculi* easy.

• *The Manarola cemetery is on...*

Punta Bonfiglio: This point offers some of the most commanding views of the entire region. To find the best vantage point, take the stairs just below the cemetery (through the green gate), then walk farther out toward the water through a park (playground, drinking water, WC, and picnic benches). Your Manarola finale is the bench at the tip of the point. Pause and take in the view. The easiest way back to town is to take the stairs at the end of the point, which join the main walking path—offering more spectacular town views on its way back to the harbor, where we started.

Sleeping in Manarola

Manarola's accommodations seem a bit more professional than the other towns (except, perhaps, Monterosso). Like the others, it has plenty of private rooms; ask in bars and restaurants.

IN THE RESIDENTIAL ZONE ABOVE THE CHURCH

This area is about a 10-minute uphill hike from the train station—just huff up the main drag to the church. All of these are within a five-minute walk from there.

$$$ La Torretta offers 11 trendy, upscale rooms (most with private deck) that cater to a demanding clientele. Probably the most elegant retreat in the region, it's a peaceful refuge with all the comforts for those happy to pay, including a communal hot tub with a view. Guests enjoy a complimentary snack and glass of prosecco on arrival, free wine tastings, an ample breakfast buffet, and a free minibar. Each chic room is distinct and described on their website (smaller Db-€170, regular Db-€200, Db suite-€300-400, 10 percent discount when you pay cash, book several months in advance, closed Dec-March, €10/day Wi-Fi includes portable device and access throughout the Cinque Terre, free baggage transfer upon request, Piazza della Chiesa beside the bell tower at Vico Volto 20, tel. 0187-920-327, www.torrettas.com, torretta@cdh.it).

$$$ B&B Da Baranin, with six good rooms and four apartments, is overpriced but nicely located just above the church (Db-€110, bigger "superior" Db-€140; apartments: Db-€120, Tb-€140, Qb-€160, no breakfast; air-con, Via Aldo Rollandi 29, tel. 0187-920-595, www.baranin.com, info@baranin.com).

$$ Aria di Mare Rooms rents four sunny rooms and an apartment 20 yards beyond Trattoria dal Billy at the very top of town. If you don't mind staying in a mostly residential zone high above the tourists, this is a great value. Three rooms have spacious terraces with knockout views and lounge chairs. Maurizio speaks a little English (Db-€85, Db apartment-€90, these prices promised through 2016, includes breakfast snacks in room, air-con, upstairs on the left at Via Aldo Rollandi 137, tel. 0187-920-367, mobile 349-058-4155, www.ariadimare.info, info@ariadimare.info, ask at Billy's if no one's home).

$ Ostello 5-Terre, Manarola's modern, pleasant hostel, occupies the former parochial school above the church square and offers

48 beds in four- to six-bed rooms. Nicola runs a calm and peaceful place—it's not a party hostel—and quiet is greatly appreciated. They rent dorm rooms as doubles with separated beds. Reserve well in advance (dorm beds-€24, Db-€65, Qb-€100; 20 percent less mid-Oct-Easter, not co-ed except for couples and families, no membership necessary, all ages, optional €2-5 breakfast, bargain dinners daily except Wed, office closed 13:00-16:00—except maybe in summer, rooms closed 10:00-13:00, check-in until 22:00, elevator, lockers, book exchange, Via B. Riccobaldi 21, tel. 0187-920-039, mobile 346-532-8078, www.hostel5terre.com, info@hostel5terre.com).

ON THE MAIN STREET

These options line up along the main street, between the harbor and the church. While in a less atmospheric area than the ones near the church, they're closer to the station—and therefore a bit handier for those packing heavy.

$$$ Albergo Ca' d'Andrean is quiet, comfortable, and chic. It has 10 big, sunny, air-conditioned rooms and a cool garden oasis complete with lemon trees. If you don't mind stairs, try requesting one of their top-floor rooms, with great views from their terraces (Sb-€95, Db-€135, Db with terrace-€155, breakfast-€7, up the hill at Via Discovolo 101, tel. 0187-920-040, www.cadandrean.it, info@cadandrean.it).

$$ At Affitta Camere da Paulin, charming Donatella and Eraldo (the town's retired policeman) rent three tasteful, tidy, well-equipped rooms with a large and inviting common living room, plus three apartments. It's in a modern setting a few minutes' walk uphill from the train tracks (Db-€110, view apartment Db-€155, Qb-€240, 3-night minimum for apartment, air-con in rooms, fans in apartments, Via Discovolo 126, mobile 334-389-4764, www.dapaulin.it, prenotazioni@dapaulin.it).

$$$ Marina Piccola offers 12 subtly stylish rooms on the water (some with sea views), but the rooms are an afterthought to their busy tourist-trap restaurant (Db-€145, air-con, Via Birolli 120, tel. 0187-920-770, www.hotelmarinapiccola.com, info@hotelmarinapiccola.com).

HIGH ABOVE MANAROLA, IN VOLASTRA

$$ Hotel il Saraceno, with seven spacious, modern, functional rooms, is a deal for drivers. Located above Manarola in the tiny town of Volastra (chock-full of vacationing Germans and Italians in summer), it's serene, clean, and right by the shuttle bus to Manarola (Db-€100, buffet breakfast, free parking, località AVA, tel. 0187-760-081, www.thesaraceno.com, hotel@thesaraceno.com, friendly Antonella).

Eating in Manarola

Restaurant options are limited in Manarola. I've listed these from lowest to highest, in terms of quality and elevation.

The vast majority of the town's restaurants (all of them decidedly touristy) are concentrated in the tight zone between Piazza Capellini and the harbor. While these are mostly interchangeable, the Scorza family works hard at **Trattoria il Porticciolo** (€7-13 pastas, €10-16 *secondi,* Thu-Tue 7:30-23:30, closed Wed, Via Birolli 92, tel. 0187-920-083). At the harborfront itself, **Marina Piccola** is famous for great views, lousy service, and price-gouging naive tourists.

Ristorante di Aristide, right on Piazza Capellini, is run by three generations of hardworking women and offers trendy atmosphere and a pleasant, less claustrophobic outdoor setting, with a view of budding soccer stars rather than harborfront glitz (€8-11 pastas, €11-20 *secondi,* €12-18 daily specials). Down the stairs, at the bottom of the main street, their simpler **café** has indoor and streetside seating, a simpler menu, and breakfast options (€5 omelettes, €7 pizzas, sandwiches, salads; Tue-Sun café open 8:00-22:30, restaurant 12:00-22:30, both closed Thu and Jan-Feb, Via Discovolo 290, tel. 0187-920-000, charming Elena, Mamma Monica, and Nonna Grazia).

Via Discovolo, the main street climbing up through town from Piazza Capellini to the church, is lined with simpler places, including a popular *gelateria* and some small grocery stores where you can browse for a picnic.

Up at the very top of town, in the residential zone above the church, dining options are sparse, but the one place that's here is a good one: **Trattoria dal Billy** offers both good food and impressive views over the valley. With Edoardo and Enrico's homemade black pasta with seafood and squid ink, green pasta with artichokes, mixed seafood starters, and homemade desserts, many find it worth the climb. Dinner reservations are a must (€8-12 pastas, €13-20 *secondi,* generally daily 12:00-15:00 & 18:00-22:00, sometimes closed Thu, Via Aldo Rollandi 122, tel. 0187-920-628, www.trattoriabilly.com). Across the street, they have an elegant, glassy dining room carved into the rock—perfect for a romantic candlelight meal with a commanding view.

Corniglia (Town #3)

This tiny, sleepy town—the only one of the five not on the water—owns a mellow main square. According to a (likely fanciful) local legend, the town was originally settled by a Roman farmer who  named it for his mother, Cornelia (how Corniglia is pronounced). The town and its ancient residents produced a wine so famous that—some say—vases found at Pompeii touted its virtues. Regardless of the veracity of the legends, wine remains Corniglia's lifeblood today. Follow the pungent smell of ripe grapes into an alley cellar and get a local to let you dip a straw into a keg.

Remote and less visited than the other Cinque Terre towns, Corniglia has fewer tourists, cooler temperatures, a few restaurants, a windy overlook on its promontory, and plenty of private rooms for rent (ask at any bar or shop, no cheaper than other towns). If you think of the Cinque Terre as the Beatles, Corniglia is Ringo.

This hilltop town has rocky sea access below its train station (toward Manarola). Once a beach, it's all been washed away—but look for signs that say *al mare* or *Marina,* where a trail leads from the town center steeply down to sunning rocks on the closest thing Corniglia has to a beach (with a shower). Corniglia's infamous Guvano beach (a bit along the coast toward Vernazza) is now essentially closed down. Created in 1893 by a landslide that cost the village a third of its farmland—and notorious throughout Italy as a nude beach—Guvano was accessed via an unused train tunnel and attracted visitors with an appetite for drug use. Now the tunnel is closed, and the national park wants people to keep their clothes on.

Thankfully, hill-capping Corniglia comes with a hardworking little shuttle bus with a reliable schedule posted both at the station and in the town. If leaving by train, review the posted shuttle schedule and time your visit to catch the bus down to conveniently arrive at the station in time for your departure. Because of the long, steep hike between the town and its train station (give yourself at least 15 minutes to rush down and catch your train, or use the shuttle bus) and Corniglia's lack of a boat dock, it's a less convenient home base for town-hopping.

Map of Corniglia:
- **1** Pan e Vin Bar (Ricci Rooms Check-In)
- **2** Il Carugio Rooms & Butiega Shop
- **3** Villa Cecio Rooms
- **4** Corniglia Hostel
- **5** Osteria Mananan & Enoteca il Pirùn
- **6** La Posada Ristorante
- **7** La Lanterna Restaurant
- **8** Gelateria

Orientation to Corniglia

TOURIST INFORMATION

A TI/park information office is at the train station (likely daily 8:00-20:00, shorter hours off-season).

ARRIVAL IN CORNIGLIA

By Train: From the station, filling a gloomy ravine far below town, a footpath zigzags up 385 steps (and nearly that many switchbacks) to the town. If you'd rather not walk, take the tiny shuttle bus—generally timed to meet arriving trains—which connects the station with Corniglia's main square, the start of my self-guided walk (€1.50 one-way at ticket office, or buy as you board for €2.50, free with Cinque Terre park card, 1-2/hour).

By Car: Only residents can park on the main road between the recommended Villa Cecio and the point where the steep switchback staircase meets the road. Beyond that area, parking is €1.50/hour. All parking areas are within an easy and fairly level walk of the town center.

Corniglia Walk

We'll explore this tiny town—population 240—and end at a scenic viewpoint. This self-guided walk might take up to 30 minutes...but only if you let yourself browse and lick a gelato cone.

• *Begin near the bus stop, located at a...*

Town Square: The gateway to this community is "Ciappà" square, with an ATM, phone booth, old wine press, and bus stop (shuttle buses timed to coordinate with train schedules). The Cinque Terre's designation as a national park sparked a revitalization of the town. Corniglia's young generation is more likely now to stay put, rather than migrate into big cities the way locals did in the past.

• *Look for the arrow pointing to the centro. Stroll the spine of Corniglia, Via Fieschi. In the fall, the smell of grapes (on their way to becoming wine) wafts from busy cellars. Along this main street, you'll see...*

Corniglia's Enticing Shops: On the right as you enter Via Fieschi, a pair of neighboring, fiercely competitive *gelaterias* jockey for your business. Both display my book, but my favorite is the second shop, **Alberto's Gelateria** (at #74). Before ordering, get a free taste of Alberto's *miele di Corniglia,* made from local honey. His lemon slush *(granita)* takes pucker to new heights.

Farther along, on the left, **Enoteca il Pirùn**—named for a type of oddly shaped old-fashioned wine pitcher designed to aerate the wine and give the alcohol more kick as you squirt it into your mouth—is located in a cool cantina at Via Fieschi 115. Sample some local wines (small tastes generally free, €3/glass). If you order wine to drink out of the *pirùn,* Mario will give you a bib. While this is a practical matter (rookies are known to dribble), it also makes a nice souvenir.

In the **Butiega** shop at Via Fieschi 142, Vincenzo sells organic local specialties (daily 8:00-19:30). For picnickers, they offer €3 made-to-order ham-and-cheese sandwiches and a fun *antipasti misti* (priced by the weight). Veronica prepares local specialties (such as pesto) daily in the shop's tiny kitchen. There are good places to picnic farther along on this walk.

• *Following Via Fieschi, you'll end up at the...*

Main Square: On Largo Taragio, tables from two bars and a trattoria spill around a WWI memorial and the town's old well. It once piped in natural spring water from the hillside to locals living without plumbing. What looks like a church is the Oratory of Santa Caterina. (An oratory is a kind of a spiritual clubhouse for a service group doing social work in the name of the Catholic Church.) Up the stairs behind the oratory, you'll find a clearing that local children have made into a soccer field. The stone benches and viewpoint make this a peaceful place for a picnic (less crowded than the end-of-town viewpoint, described next).

• *Opposite the oratory, notice how steps lead steeply down on Via alla Marina to Corniglia's non-beach. It's a five-minute paved climb to sunning rocks, a shower, and a small deck (with a treacherous entry into the water). From the square, continue up Via Fieschi to the...*

End-of-Town Viewpoint: The Santa Maria Belvedere, named for a church that once stood here, marks the scenic end of Corniglia. This is a super picnic spot. From here, look high to the west (right), where the village and sanctuary of San Bernardino straddle a ridge (a good starting point for a hike; accessible by shuttle bus from Monterosso or a long uphill hike from Vernazza). Below is the tortuous harbor, where locals hoist their boats onto the cruel rocks.

Sleeping in Corniglia

Perched high above the sea on a hilltop, Corniglia has plenty of private rooms. To get to the town from the station, catch the shuttle bus or make the 15-minute uphill hike. The town is riddled with humble places that charge too much (generally Db-€65) and have meager business skills and a limited ability to converse with tourists—so it's almost never full.

$$ Cristiana Ricci is an exception to the rule. She communicates well and is reliable, renting three small, clean, and peaceful rooms—one with a terrace and sweeping view—just inland from the bus stop (Db-€60-70, Tb-€80, Qb-€90, €10/day less when you stay 2 or more nights, check in at the Pan e Vin bar at Via Fieschi 123, mobile 338-937-6547, cri_affittacamere@virgilio.it). She also rents three big, modern apartments (€90 for 2-4 people).

$$ Il Carugio has nine modern, sunny rooms right in the center of the village, most with sea views. The communal rooftop terrace offers a commanding view of the coast (Db-€70, Db with seaview balcony-€85, Db apartment-€90 plus €15/extra person, air-con, no breakfast, free parking, free self-serve laundry, tel. 0187-812-293, mobile 335-175-7946 or 329-228-3803, www.ilcarugiodicorniglia.com, info@ilcarugiodicorniglia.com, Lidia).

$$ Villa Cecio (pronounced "chay-choh") feels like an abandoned hotel. They offer eight well-worn rooms on the outskirts of town, with saggy beds and little character or warmth. Some rooms have great views, and three have terraces—worth requesting when you check in. All of the rooms share a big rooftop terrace with a grand view (Db-€70 promised in 2016, breakfast-€5, four rooms have air-con, on main road 200 yards toward Vernazza at Via Serra 58, tel. 0187-812-043, mobile 334-350-6637, www.cecio5terre.com, info@cecio5terre.com, Giacinto). They also rent eight similar rooms (Db-€65, view Db-€70) in an annex on the square where the bus stops.

$ Corniglia Hostel was formerly the town's schoolhouse. It rents 24 beds in a pastel-yellow building up some steps from the square where the bus stops. The playground in front is often busy with happy kids. Despite its strict and institutional atmosphere, the hostel's prices, central location, and bright, clean rooms ensure its popularity. Its hotelesque double rooms are open to anyone (bunk in dorm room-€24, three Db-€55—€60 July-Aug, one private Qb-€100, breakfast-€5, office open 7:00-13:00 & 15:00-1:30 in the morning, dorms closed 10:30-15:00, private rooms closed 13:00-15:00, 1:30 curfew, air-con, lockers, €5 self-serve laundry, Via alla Stazione 3, tel. 0187-812-559, www. ostellocorniglia.com, ostellocorniglia@gmail.com, Andrea, Alessandro, and Elisabetta).

Eating in Corniglia

Corniglia has few restaurants. The typical array of pizzerias, *focaccerias,* and *alimentari* (grocery stores) line the narrow main drag. For a real meal, consider one of these options.

Osteria Mananan—between the Ciappà bus stop and the main square at Via Fieschi 117—serves what many consider the best food in town in its small, stony, elegant interior (€10 pastas, €10-16 *secondi,* Wed-Mon 12:30-14:30 & 19:30-22:00, closed Tue, no outdoor seating, tel. 0187-821-166).

Enoteca il Pirùn, next door on Via Fieschi, has a small restaurant above the wine bar, where Mario serves typical local dishes (€8-10 pastas, €10-16 *secondi,* €28 fixed-price meal includes homemade wine, daily 12:00-16:00 & 19:30-23:30, tel. 0187-812-315).

La Posada Ristorante offers dinner in a garden under trees, overlooking the Ligurian Sea. To get here, stroll out of town to the top of the stairs that lead down to the station (€8-10 pastas, €10-16 *secondi,* €18 tourist fixed-price meal, daily 12:00-16:00 & 19:00-23:00, tel. 0187-821-174, mobile 338-232-5734).

The trattoria **La Lanterna,** on the main square, is the most atmospheric, but without particularly charming service (€10-14 pastas, €10-18 *secondi,* daily 12:00-15:00 & 19:30-21:30).

Vernazza (Town #4)

With the closest thing to a natural harbor—overseen by a ruined castle and a stout stone church—Vernazza is the jewel of the Cinque Terre. Only the occasional noisy slurping up of the train by the mountain reminds you of the modern world.

CINQUE TERRE

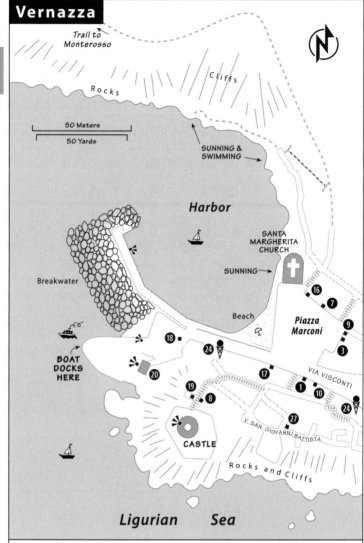

Vernazza

Trail to Monterosso

Cliffs

Rocks

50 Meters
50 Yards

SUNNING & SWIMMING

Harbor

SANTA MARGHERITA CHURCH

SUNNING →

Breakwater

Beach

Piazza Marconi

BOAT DOCKS HERE

VIA VISCONTI

V. SAN GIOVANNI / BATTISTA

CASTLE

Rocks and Cliffs

Ligurian Sea

❶ Gianni Franzi Reception/Ristorante

❷ Pensione Sorriso

❸ Albergo Barbara Rooms & Francamaria Reception

❹ La Perla delle 5 Terre Rooms, Tonino Basso Rooms & Il Pirata delle Cinque Terre Café

❺ Camere Fontana Vecchia

❻ Giuliano Basso Rooms

❼ Martina Callo Rooms, Capitano Rooms Reception & Trattoria del Capitano

❽ Monica Lercari Rooms

❾ Nicolina Rooms Reception & Ristorante Pizzeria Vulnetia

❿ Rosa Vitali Rooms

⓫ Vernazza Rooms Reception & Blue Marlin Bar

⓬ Rooms Francesca Reception (Enoteca Sciacchetrà)

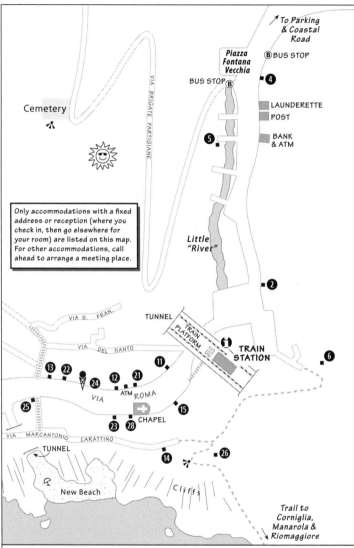

Only accommodations with a fixed address or reception (where you check in, then go elsewhere for your room) are listed on this map. For other accommodations, call ahead to arrange a meeting place.

⑬ Ivo's Camere Reception (Pizzeria Fratelli Basso)

⑭ Rooms Elisabetta (call first)

⑮ Eva's Rooms & Trattoria da Sandro

⑯ Ananasso Bar

⑰ Gambero Rosso Ristorante

⑱ Pizzeria Baia Saracena

⑲ Ristorante al Castello

⑳ Ristorante Belforte

㉑ Antica Osteria il Baretto

㉒ Forno Bakery

㉓ Lunch Box

㉔ Gelaterias (3)

㉕ Internet Point

㉖ Franco's Ristorante & Bar la Torre

㉗ Vernazza Wine Experience

㉘ Vineria Santa Marta

The action is at the harbor, where you'll find outdoor restaurants, a bar hanging on the edge of the castle, and a breakwater with a promenade, corralled by a natural amphitheater of terraced hills. In the summer, the beach becomes a soccer field, with teams fielded by local bars and restaurants providing late-night entertainment. In the dark, locals fish off the promontory, using glowing bobbers that shine in the waves.

Proud of their Vernazzan heritage, the town's 500 residents like to brag: "Vernazza is locally owned. Portofino has sold out." Fearing the change it would bring, keep-Vernazza-small proponents stopped the construction of a major road into the town and region. Families are tight and go back centuries; several generations live together. In the winter, the population shrinks, as many people return to their more comfortable big-city apartments to spend the money they reaped during the tourist season.

Although Vernazza was hit harder than any other Cinque Terre town by the 2011 flood (see sidebar), things are now back to normal. Leisure time is devoted to taking part in the *passeggiata*—strolling lazily together up and down the main street and complaining about the newly renovated harbor square. A fancy 2014 project replaced the benches, lamps, landscaping, and, most importantly, reworked the drainage system underneath. As is generally the case, change is hard to swallow until you get used to it. Sit on a bench and study the passersby doing their *vasche* (laps). Explore the characteristic alleys, called *carugi*. Learn—and live—the phrase *"la vita pigra di Vernazza"* (the lazy life of Vernazza).

Orientation to Vernazza

TOURIST INFORMATION

Two information points at the train station face each other across the platform: the gift shop, where you can get answers to basic questions (daily 8:00-20:00, closed in winter), and the train ticket desk/park office (likely daily 8:00-20:00, shorter hours off-season, tel. 0187-812-533). Public WCs are just behind.

ARRIVAL IN VERNAZZA

By Train: Vernazza's train station is only about three train cars long, but the trains are much longer—so most of the cars come to a stop in a long, dark tunnel. Get out anyway, and walk through the tunnel to the station. From there the main drag flows through town right to the harbor.

By Car: Roads to Vernazza are in terrible shape, and parking is strictly limited. The best advice: Don't drive to Vernazza. If you're coming from the north, park in Levanto. If arriving from the south, park your car in La Spezia. From those towns, hop on the train.

If you must drive, get precise advice from your hotelier about which roads are open, how to drive in, and where to park (see "Cinque Terre Connections" at the end of this chapter). Yellow lines mark parking spots for residents only.

HELPFUL HINTS

Internet Access: The slick, expensive, **Internet Point,** run by Alberto and Isabella, is in the village center (daily June-Oct 9:30-23:00, until 20:00 Nov-May). The **Il Pirata delle Cinque Terre** bar (behind/above the train station) and **Blue Marlin Bar** (along the main street) both offer free Wi-Fi with a purchase.

Baggage Storage: You can leave your bags at the train-station gift shop (near track 1). Bags are kept in a secure room below the tracks on the main street, but you can only access them during shop hours (€1/hour, €10/day, daily 8:00-20:00, closed in winter). Friendly Francesco and his staff will happily take your luggage from the train station to your hotel—and back (€2-3/piece).

Laundry: The small self-serve launderette is at the top of town next to the post office (coin-op, €5/wash, €5/dry, includes soap, daily 7:00-23:00, operated by Domenico and Barbara at the fish shop). As it can be busy, consider the full-service laundry in Monterosso, which offers a more efficient "drop off and pick up later" service.

Massage: Kate Allen offers a super-relaxing fusion of aromatic/Swedish/holistic massage in her little studio in the center across from the pharmacy (€60/hour, tel. 0187-812-537, mobile 333-568-4653, www.vernazzamassage5terre.com).

Best Views: A steep 10-minute hike in either direction from Vernazza gives you a classic village photo op. For the best light, head toward Corniglia in the morning—best views are just before the ticket booth for the national park—and toward Monterosso in the evening—best views are after the ticket booth.

Vernazza Walk

This self-guided walk includes Vernazza's characteristic town squares and ends on its scenic breakwater.

• *From the train station, walk uphill along the stream until you hit the small square in front of the Il Pirata delle Cinque Terre café, near the post office. This part of town was damaged during the flood, but is now being repaired. The stream in this ravine once powered Vernazza's water mill. Shuttle buses run from here to hamlets and sanctuaries in the hills above.*

Walk to the tidy, modern square called...

Fontana Vecchia: Named after a long-gone fountain, this is where older locals remember the river filled with townswomen doing their washing. A steep lane leads from here up to the cemetery (20-minute hike) and to the sanctuary beyond that (1-hour hike). It's marked by an icon of Madonna di Reggio, beloved by the people of Vernazza. Imagine the entire village sadly trudging up here during funerals. (The cemetery is peaceful and evocative at sunset, when the fading light touches each crypt.)

You may see some construction work going on here. Following the 2011 flood, Vernazza attracted worldwide sympathy—including that of prominent architect Richard Rogers (who designed London's Millennium Dome and, with frequent collaborator Renzo Piano, Paris' Pompidou Centre). Having enjoyed many relaxing summer vacations in Vernazza, Rogers wanted to give something back. He helped redesign the spine of the town, from here down the main street to the harborfront square (basically the route of this walk). Over the next several years, his plans will help reshape Vernazza—making it more up-to-date, but keeping its traditional soul.

• *Begin your saunter downhill to the harbor. Just before the* Pensione Sorriso *sign, on your right (at #7, with big brown garage doors and a* croce verde Vernazza *sign), you'll see the...*

Ambulance Barn: A group of volunteers is always on call for a dash to the hospital, 40 minutes away in La Spezia. Opposite the barn is a big empty lot. Like many landowners, the owner of Pensione Sorriso had plans to expand, but since the 1980s, the government has said "No." While some landowners are frustrated, the old character of these towns survives. A few steps farther down is the town clinic. The *guarda medica* (emergency doctor—see buzzer) sleeps upstairs.

• *At the corner across from the playground, on a marble plaque in the wall on the left, you'll see a...*

World Wars Monument: This is dedicated to those killed in World Wars I and II. Not a family in Vernazza was spared. Listed on the left are soldiers *morti in combattimento,* who died in World War I; on the right is the WWII section. Some were deported to *Germania;* others—labeled *Part* (for *partigiani,* or partisans, generally communists)—were killed while fighting against Mussolini. Cynics considered partisans less than heroes. After 1943, Hitler called up Italian boys over 15. Rather than die on the front for Hitler, they escaped to the hills and became "resistance fighters" in order to remain free.

The path to Corniglia leaves from here (behind and above

The Cinque Terre Flood and Recovery

On October 25, 2011, after a very dry summer, a freak rainstorm hit the Cinque Terre. Within four hours, 22 inches of rain fell. Flash floods rushed down the hillsides. Topography al-

lowed the water to quickly drain in Riomaggiore, Manarola, and Corniglia, which were mostly undamaged. But Monterosso and Vernazza were devastated, with much of the two towns buried under 10 feet of mud and left without water, electricity, or phone connections.

The destruction occurred mostly along former ravines, where, historically, streams ran through the towns. In the last century, the ravines were covered with roads, and the streams channeled into underground canals that, over time, were not properly maintained. Like congested arteries, the drainage canals couldn't handle the raging flow. Water pressure caused streets to explode upward. Medieval wells in basements became geysers. Rivers of raging mud carrying rocks, trees, furniture, and even cars and buses rampaged down the main streets, burying the shops and restaurants of old Monterosso and Vernazza. Four villagers lost their lives. (For a sense of the horror of this disaster and the power of the raging water tearing through the villages, search for videos of the "Cinque Terre 2011 flood" on YouTube.)

The people of the Cinque Terre were taught a tough lesson. It's their beautiful land that brings the tourists. But with the affluence brought by tourism, some had abandoned their land—leaving vineyards unplanted and centuries-old drystone terracing to crumble—for less physically demanding, more profitable work in town. (Grapevines have far-reaching root systems that help combat erosion, and traditional vintners keep their stone terraces in good order.) After a generation of neglect, the unprotected land was washed down into the towns by the violent weather.

Today, you'll find the Cinque Terre is back to normal. You may not even realize that in the affected areas of Vernazza and Monterosso, everything is brand-new: stoves, tables, chairs, plates, walls lined with bottles of wine, and so on, all had to be replaced from scratch. Strolling through these towns today, keep in mind everything these people have been through—and appreciate the resilience of the human spirit.

the plaque). Behind you is a small square, decorated with big millstones, once used to grind local olives into oil. There's a good chance you'll see an expat mom here at the village playground with her kids. I've met many American women who fell in love with a local guy, stayed, and are now happily raising families here. (But I've rarely met an American guy who moved in with a local girl.)

From here, Vernazza's tiny river goes underground. Until the 1950s, the river ran openly through the center of town. Old-timers recall the days before the breakwater, when the river cascaded down and the surf sent waves rolling up Vernazza's main drag. (The name "Vernazza" is actually local dialect for "little Venice"—before the main road covered up the stream, the town had a string of charming bridges, evoking those in Venice.)

Corralling this stream under the modern street, and forcing it to take a hard right turn here, contributed to the damage caused by the 2011 flood. After the flood, alpine engineers were imported from Switzerland to redesign the drainage system, so any future floods will be less destructive. They also installed nets above the town to protect it from landslides.

Just before the tracks, panels provide limited space for advertising for each political party. The walls under the tracks serve as a sort of community information center. The bulletin board on the right lists local volunteers and when they are on call to drive the ambulance.

The second set of train tracks (nearer the harbor) was recently renovated to lessen disruptive noise, but locals say it made no difference. At the base of the stairs a TV monitor displays information for arriving and departing trains (it's very handy, as printed schedules are hard to rely on).

On the left, just past the tracks, you'll see a giant poster with photos of the 2011 flood *(alluvione)* and the shops that it devastated. "The 25th of October" is a day that will live forever in this town's lore. Vernazza is built around one street—basically a lid over the stream in its ravine. On that fateful day, the surrounding hills acted like a funnel, directing flash-flood waters right through the middle of town. As you stroll from here to the harbor, imagine this street buried under 13 feet of mud. Every shop, restaurant, and hotel on the main drag had to be rewired, replumbed, and re-equipped.

• *Follow the road downhill to...*

Vernazza's "Commercial Center": Here, you'll pass many locals doing their *vasche* (laps). Next, you'll pass souvenir shops, wine shops, the Blue Marlin Bar (Vernazza's top nightspot), and the tiny Chapel of Santa Marta (the small stone chapel with iron grillwork over the window, on the left), where Mass is celebrated only on special Sundays. Above and behind the chapel is the Vineria Santa

Marta wine bar. Farther down, you'll walk by a *gelateria,* bakery, pharmacy, a grocery, and another *gelateria.* There are plenty of fun and cheap food-to-go options here.

• *On the left, in front of the second* gelateria, *a stone arch was blasted away by the 2011 flood. Scamper through the hole in the rock to reach Vernazza's shrinking...*

"**New Beach**": This is where the town's stream used to hit the sea back in the 1970s. Older locals remember frolicking on a beach

here when they were kids, but the constant, churning surf eventually eroded it all the way back to the cliff. When the 2011 flood hit, it blew out the passageway and deposited landslide material here from the hills above. In the flood's aftermath, Vernazza's main drag and harbor were filled with mud and silt. Workers used the debris to fill in even more of this beach, and for several years Vernazza had a popular beach that felt a world away from the bustle of the main drag. But as time goes on, the forces of nature are once again taking it away.

• *Back on the main drag, continue downhill to the...*

Harbor Square (Piazza Marconi) and Breakwater: Vernazza, with the only natural harbor of the Cinque Terre, was established as the sole place boats could pick up the fine local wine. The two-foot-high square stone at the foot of the stairs (on the left) is marked *Sasso del Sego* (stone of tallow). Workers crushed animal flesh and fat in its basin to make tallow, which drained out of the tiny hole below. The tallow was then used to waterproof boats or wine barrels. Stonework is the soul of the region. Take some time to appreciate the impressive stonework of the restaurant interiors facing the harbor.

On the far side (behind Ristorante Pizzeria Vulnetia), peek into the tiny street with its commotion of arches. Vernazza's most characteristic side streets, called *carugi,* lead up from here. The narrow stairs mark the beginning of the trail that leads up, up, up to the quintessential view of Vernazza—and, eventually, on to Monterosso.

Located in front of the harborside church, the tiny piazza—decorated with a river-rock mosaic—is a popular hangout spot. It's where Vernazza's old ladies soak up the last bit of sun, and kids enjoy a patch of level ball field.

Vernazza's harborfront **church** is unusual for its strange entryway, which faces east (altar side), rather than the more typical western orientation. With relative peace and prosperity in the 16th century, the townspeople doubled the church in size, causing it to overtake a little piazza that once faced the west facade. From the square, use the "new" entry and climb the steps, keeping an eye out for the level necessary to keep the church high and dry. Inside, the lighter pillars in the back mark the 16th-century extension. Three historic portable crosses hanging on the walls are carried through town during religious holiday processions. They are replicas of crosses that (locals like to believe) Vernazza ships once carried on crusades to the Holy Land. In 1998, Vernazza's priest was gruesomely and mysteriously murdered. While circumstantial evidence points to fascinating conspiracy theories, no one knows whodunit (or, at least, no one's telling). Today's priest, Don Giovanni, is popular—he stopped the church bells from ringing through the night (light sleepers rejoiced). In the wake of the 2011 flood, he opened up the church as a staging ground for recovery services.

• *Finish your town tour seated out on the breakwater (perhaps with a glass of local white wine or something more interesting from a nearby bar—borrow the glass, they don't mind). Face the town, and see...*

The Harbor: In a moderate storm, you'd be soaked, as waves routinely crash over the *molo* (breakwater, built in 1972). Waves can rearrange the huge rocks—depositing them from the breakwater onto the piazza and its benches. Freak waves have even washed away tourists squinting excitedly into their cameras. (I've seen it happen.) In 2007, an American woman was swept away and killed by a rogue wave. Enjoy the waterfront piazza—carefully.

The train line (to your left) was constructed in 1874 to tie together a newly united Italy, and linked Turin and Genoa with Rome. A second line (hidden in a tunnel at this point) was built in the 1920s. The yellow building alongside the tracks was Vernazza's first train station. Along the wall behind the tracks, you can see the four bricked-up alcoves where people once waited for trains. Notice the wonderful concrete sunbathing strip (and place for late-night privacy) laid below the tracks along the rocks.

Vernazza's fishing fleet is down to just a few boats (with the net spools). Vernazzans are still more likely to own a boat than a car, and it's said that you stand a better chance of surviving if you mess with a local man's wife than with his boat.

Boats are on buoys, except in winter or when the red storm flag (see the pole at the start of the breakwater) indicates bad seas. At these times, the boats are pulled up onto the square—which is usually reserved for restaurant tables. In the 1970s, tiny Vernazza had one of Italy's top water polo teams, and the harbor was their "pool." Later, when the league required a real pool, Vernazza dropped out.

The Castle (Castello Doria): On the far right, the castle, which is now a grassy park with great views (and nothing but stones), still guards the town (€1.50 donation, daily 10:00-18:30; from harbor, take stairs by Trattoria Gianni and follow *Ristorante al Castello* signs, tower is a few steps beyond). This was the town's watchtower back in pirate days, and a Nazi lookout in World War II. The castle tower looks new because it was rebuilt

after the British bombed it, chasing out the Germans. The squat tower on the water is a great spot for a glass of wine or a meal. From the breakwater, you could follow the rope to Ristorante Belforte and pop inside, past the actual submarine door. A photo of a major storm showing the entire tower under a wave (not uncommon in the winter) hangs near the bar.

The Town: Before the 12th century, pirates made the coast uninhabitable, so the first Vernazzans lived in the hills above (near the Reggio Sanctuary). The town itself—and its towers, fortified walls, and hillside terracing—are mostly from the 12th through the 15th century, when Vernazza was allied with the Republic of Genoa.

Vernazza has two halves. *Sciuiu* (Vernazzan dialect for "flowery") is the sunny side on the left, and *luvegu* (dank) is the shady side on the right. Houses below the castle were connected by an interior arcade—ideal for fleeing attacks. The "Ligurian pastel" colors are regulated by a commissioner of good taste in the regional government. The square before you is locally famous for some of the area's finest restaurants. The big red central house—on the site where Genoan warships were built in the 12th century—used to be a guardhouse.

In the Middle Ages, there was no beach or square. The water went right up to the buildings, where boats would tie up, Venetian-style. Imagine what Vernazza looked like in those days, when it was the biggest and richest of the Cinque Terre towns. Buildings had a water gate (facing today's square) and a front door on the higher inland side. There was no pastel plaster—just fine stonework (traces of which survive above the Trattoria del Capitano). Apart from the added plaster, the general shape and size of the town has changed little in five centuries. Survey the windows and notice inhabitants quietly gazing back.

While the town has 1,500 residents in summer, only 500 stay here through the winter. Vernazza has accommodations for about 500 tourists.

Above the Town: The small, round tower above the red guardhouse—another part of the city fortifications—reminds us of the town's importance in the Middle Ages. Back then, its key ally Genoa's enemies (i.e., the other maritime republics, especially Pisa) were Vernazza's enemies. Franco's Ristorante and Bar la Torre, just above and beyond the tower, welcomes hikers who are finishing, starting, or simply contemplating the Corniglia-Vernazza hike, with great town views. That tower recalls a time when the entire town was fortified by a stone wall.

Vineyards fill the mountainside beyond the town. Notice the many terraces. Someone—probably after too much of that local wine—calculated that the roughly 3,000 miles of dry-stone walls built to terrace the region's vineyards have the same amount of stonework as the Great Wall of China.

For six centuries, the economy was based on wine and olive oil. Then came the 1980s—and the tourists. Locals turned to tourism to make a living, and stopped tending the land. Many vineyards were abandoned, and the terraces fell into disrepair. But it's the stonework of the terracing in the surrounding hills that helps prevent flooding—a lesson learned in the worst possible way in 2011.

Although many locals still maintain their tiny plots and proudly serve their family wines, the patchwork of local vineyards is atomized and complex because of inheritance traditions. Historically, families divided their land among their children. Parents wanted each child to get some good land. Because some lots were "kissed by the sun" while others were shady, the lots were split into increasingly tiny and eventually unviable pieces—another reason why many have been abandoned.

A single steel train line winds up the gully behind the tower. It is for the vintner's *trenino,* the tiny service train. Play "Where's *trenino?*" and see if you can find two trains. The vineyards once stretched as high as you can see, but since fewer people sweat in the fields these days, the most distant terraces have gone wild again.

The Church, School, and City Hall: Vernazza's Ligurian Gothic church, built with black stones quarried from Punta Mesco (the distant point behind you), dates from 1318. Note the gray stone that marks the church's 16th-century expansion. The gray-and-red house above the spire is the local elementary school (about 25 children attend; education through age 16 is obligatory). Older students go to the "big city," La Spezia. The red building to the right of the schoolhouse, a former monastery, is the city hall. Vernazza and Corniglia function as one community. Through most of the 1990s, the local government was Communist. In 1999, residents elected a coalition of many parties working to rise above ideologies and simply make Vernazza a better place. That practical notion of government continues here today.

Finally, on the top of the hill, with the best view of all, is the town cemetery. It's only fair that hardworking Vernazzans—who spend their lives climbing up and down and up and down and up and down the hillsides that hem in their little town—are rewarded with a world-class view from their eternal resting place.

Experiences in Vernazza

Tuesday-Morning Market

Vernazza's skimpy business community is augmented Tuesday mornings (8:00-13:00), when a meager gang of cars and trucks pulls into town for a tailgate market. Eros is often among the vendors; his family has sold flowers here for years (and he's also an amazing opera singer).

Beaches

The harbor's sandy cove has sunning rocks and showers by the breakwater. There's also a ladder on the breakwater for deep-water access. The sunbathing lane directly under the church has a shower. And, while it's getting smaller and rockier each year, Vernazza's "new beach" can be accessed through a hole halfway along its main drag.

Boat Rides

From the harbor, boats run nearly hourly (10:30-17:00) to Monterosso, Manarola, Riomaggiore, and Portovenere. Schedules are posted in Cinque Terre park offices.

Private Boat Trips

Vincenzo of **Nord Est** takes people out for mini-cruises (€150/hour, mobile 338-700-0436, info@nordest-vernazza.com). One popular stop is the tiny *acqua pendente* (waterfall) cove between Vernazza and Monterosso; locals call it their *laguna blu*.

Vernazza Water Taxi can take you directly to any Cinque Terre town and beyond in Pietro's 10-person boat. Prices vary depending on distance (one-way to Monterroso-€30, one-way to Riomaggiore-€50; €5 extra/person). You can also arrange pickup from any town, baggage transport, and tours.

Shuttle Bus Joyride

For a cheap and scenic joyride, with a chance to chat about the region with friendly, English-speaking Beppe, Simone, Mirco, or Pietro, ride the shuttle bus from the top of town (in front of the post office) to the sanctuaries and hamlets above town, including San Bernadino, and back again (entire route for the cost of a round-trip ticket, generally about 5/day, but times are very unpredictable—

CINQUE TERRE

try asking at the TI or park office in the train station, or if you see a bus, ask for the timetable; free with Cinque Terre park card, churches at sanctuaries are usually closed).

Sustainable Tourism Activities

Save Vernazza, which began as a post-flood relief organization, has evolved into an all-purpose Vernazza advocacy group, with an emphasis on fostering sustainable tourism. If you enjoy the Cinque Terre and would like to give something back, contact them to participate in a project designed to protect and promote Vernazza. Their "voluntourism" activities, scheduled regularly through the high season, include rebuilding terrace walls and harvesting grapes (reservations required, lunch and wine provided, generally 2/week late May-Oct 8:30-13:30, see website for schedule, www. savevernazza.com, workwithus@savevernazza.com, mobile 349-357-3572, Michelle and Ruth).

Sleeping in Vernazza

Vernazza, the spindly and salty essence of the Cinque Terre, is my top choice for a home base. Off-season (Oct-March), you can generally arrive without a reservation and find a place, but at other times, it's smart to book ahead (especially June-July and weekends).

People recommended here are listed for their communication skills (they speak English, have email, and are reliable with bookings) and because they rent several rooms. Consequently, my recommendations cost more than comparable rooms you'll find if you shop around. Comparison-shopping will likely save you €10-20 per double per night—and often get you a better place and view to boot. The real Vernazza gems are stray single rooms with owners who have no interest in booking in advance or messing with email. Arrive by early afternoon and drop by any shop or bar and ask; most locals know someone who rents rooms.

Anywhere you stay here requires some climbing, but keep in mind that more climbing means better views. Most do not include breakfast (for suggestions, see "Eating in Vernazza," later). Cash is preferred or required almost everywhere. Night noise can be a problem if you're near the station. Rooms on the harbor come with church bells (but only between 7:00 and 22:00).

PENSIONS

$$$ Gianni Franzi, a busy restaurant on the harbor square, rents 25 small rooms. The rooms are in three buildings—one funky, two modern—up a hundred tight, winding spiral stairs. The funky ones, which may or may not have private baths, are artfully decorated à la shipwreck, with tiny balconies and grand sea views *(con vista sul mare)*.

The comfy new *(nuovo)* rooms lack views. Both have modern bathrooms and access to a super-scenic cliff-hanging guests' garden. Steely Marisa requires check-in before 16:00 or a phone call to explain when you're coming. Emanuele (Gianni's son, who runs the restaurant), Simona, Caterina, and the staff speak a little English (S-€55, D-€110, Db-€130, Tb-€160, view room-€20-30 extra, includes breakfast on gorgeous seaview terrace mid-April–mid-Oct, lower prices at other times, 10  percent discount in 2016 when you pay cash and mention this book—request when you reserve, cancellations less than a week in advance charged one night's deposit, closed Jan-Feb, Piazza Marconi 1, tel. 0187-812-228, tel. 0187-821-003, on Wed call mobile 393-9008-155, www.giannifranzi.it, info@giannifranzi.it). Pick up your keys at Gianni Franzi restaurant on the harbor square (on Wed, when the restaurant is closed, call ahead to make other arrangements).

$$$ Pensione Sorriso, the oldest pension in town (where I stayed on my first visit in 1975), rents 13 overpriced, tired rooms above the train station. While the building has charm, it comes with train noise and saggy beds (Sb-€65, D-€70, Db-€110, Db with air-con-€120, T-€90, Tb-€140, breakfast-€10, closed Nov-March, Via Gavino 4, tel. 0187-812-224, www.pensionesorriso.com, info@pensionesorriso.com, Francesca and Aldo).

$$ Albergo Barbara rents nine basic rooms overlooking the harbor square—most with small windows and small views. It's run by English-speaking Giuseppe and his no-nonsense Swiss wife, Patricia (D-€60, D with private bath down the hall-€70, Db-€80, big Db with nice harbor view-€120, extra bed-€10, 2-night stay preferred, closed Dec-Feb, reserve online with credit card but pay cash, Piazza Marconi 30, tel. 0187-812-398, mobile 338-793-3261, www.albergobarbara.it, info@albergobarbara.it).

PRIVATE ROOMS (AFFITTA CAMERE)

Vernazza is honeycombed with private rooms, offering the best values in town. Owners may be reluctant to reserve rooms far in advance. Doubles cost €55-120, depending on the view, season, and plumbing—you get what you pay for. Apartments (with kitchens) go for a bit more. Most places accept only cash. Some have killer views, come with lots of stairs, and cost the same as a small, dark place on a back lane over the train tracks. Most owners speak just enough English (or know someone who does).

While a few places have all their beds in one building, most have rooms scattered over town. Better-organized outfits have an informal "reception desk" (sometimes at a restaurant or other business) where you can check in. A few places have no reception at all. (On the Vernazza map, I've marked only places that have a fixed address or reception office; if I say "reception," you'll check in there, then continue on to your actual room.) Because this can be confusing, I strongly recommend clearly communicating your arrival time (by phone or email) and getting clear instructions on where to meet the owner and pick up the keys. In many cases, they'll meet you at the train station—but only if they know when you're coming.

Well-Run Rooms in the Inland Part of Town

Some of my favorite places in town are located in the ravine a five-minute, gently uphill stroll behind the train station. While this sleepy zone is less atmospheric and feels less central than Vernazza's main street, harborfront, and twisty upper lanes, it also has less train and church-bell noise and fewer steep stairs. While none of these places have views, the constant soundtrack of Vernazza's gurgling river is soothing. Il Pirata delle Cinque Terre is the neighborhood hub (offering breakfast and Wi-Fi), and Vernazza's tiny self-service launderette is right next door.

$$$ Alessandra runs two different sets of rooms in a single elevator-equipped, modern building: **La Perla delle 5 Terre** (6 clean, sleek rooms with bohemian-chic style but no air-con, Db-€100, Tb-€120) and **Tonino Basso** (4 rooms decorated with big colorful cutouts, Db-€120, Tb-€140, air-con). This is a top choice in town for modern comfort—at a steep price. La Perla is a better value if you don't need air-conditioning (contact for both: Via Gavino 34, mobile 339-761-1651, www.toninobasso.com, sassarinialessandra@libero.it).

$$ **Camere Fontana Vecchia,** run by Annamaria, has eight bright, spacious, quiet rooms overlooking the ravine and its rushing river, across the street from the post office (D-€70, Db-€80, three Db with terrace-€100, Via Gavino 15, tel. 0187-821-130, mobile 333-454-9371, www.cinqueterrecamere.com, m.annamaria@libero.it).

$$ **Giuliano Basso**'s four carefully crafted rooms are just above town, straddling a ravine among orange trees. It's proudly built out of stone by Giuliano himself—the town's last stone-layer (Db-€80-100, Tb-€120, two rooms have air-con, more train noise than others, above train station—take the ramp just before Pensione Sorriso, mobile 333-341-4792, www.cdh.it/giuliano, giuliano@cdh.it).

$$ **La Rosa dei Venti** (The Compass Rose), run by Giuliana Basso, houses three tranquil, airy rooms in her childhood home at the top of town, three floors up from the ravine. One room has a balcony. Call to arrange a meeting time (Db-€80, Tb-€110, Via Gavino 19, tel. 333-762-4679, info@larosadeiventi-vernazza.it).

Other Reliable Places Scattered Through Town and the Harborside

La Malà, La Marina Rooms, and Memo Rooms are not located on the map in this chapter; arrange a meeting time and/or ask for directions when you reserve.

$$$ La Malà is Vernazza's jet-setter pad. Four pristine white rooms boast fancy-hotel-type extras and a common seaview terrace. It's a climb—way up to the top of town—but they'll carry your bags to and from the station (Db-€160, Db suite-€220, includes breakfast at a bar, air-con, mobile 334-287-5718, www.lamala.it, info@lamala.it, charming Giamba and his mama, Armanda). They also rent the simpler "Armanda's Room" nearby—a great value, since you get Giamba's attention to detail and amenities without paying for a big view (Db-€80, includes simple breakfast, air-con).

$$$ La Marina Rooms is run by hardworking Christian, who speaks English and happily meets guests at the station to carry their bags. There are five beautiful, top-end, pricey units, most high above the main street: One single works as a tight double, and three doubles share a fine oceanview terrace (town view Sb-€60, Db-€110, seaview Db-€150), and two spacious apartments with fine terraces and views (town-view Db-€120, seaview 2-bedroom apartment with big terrace-€260; mobile 338-476-7472, www.lamarinarooms.com, mapcri@yahoo.it).

$$$ Martina Callo's four simply furnished rooms overlook the square; they're up plenty of steps near the silent-at-night church tower. While the rooms are nothing special, guests pay for and appreciate the views (room #1: Tb-€120 or Qb-€130 with harbor view; room #2: big Qb family room with no view-€120; room #3: Db with grand view terrace-€100; room #4: roomy Db with no view-€60; air-con, ring bell at Piazza Marconi 26, tel. 0187-812-365, mobile 329-435-5344, www.roomartina.it, roomartina@roomartina.it).

$$ Memo Rooms rents three clean and spacious rooms overlooking the main street, in what feels like a miniature hotel. Enrica will meet you if you call upon arrival (Db-€70, Via Roma 15, try Enrica's mobile first at 338-285-2385, otherwise tel. 0187-812-360, www.memorooms.com, info@memorooms.com).

$$ Monica Lercari rents several rooms with modern comforts, perched at the top of town (small Db-€80, seaview D-€100, grand seaview terrace D-€120, includes breakfast, air-con, tel. 0187-812-296, mobile 320-025-4515, alcastellovernazza@yahoo.it). Monica and her husband, Massimo, run the Ristorante al Castello, in the old castle tower overlooking town.

$$ Nicolina Rooms consists of seven units in three different buildings. Two rooms are in the center over the pharmacy, up a few steep steps (Db-€90); another room is on a twisty lane above the harbor (large studio Db with terrace-€200); and four more are in a building beyond the church, with great views (D-€100, Db-€140, two-bedroom suite with harbor view-€180 plus €30/extra person, Wi-Fi and loud church bells in these rooms only). Inquire at Pizzeria Vulnetia on the harbor square (all include breakfast, Piazza Marconi 29, tel. 0187-821-193, mobile 333-842-6879, www.camerenicolina.it, camerenicolina.info@cdh.it).

$$ Rosa Vitali rents two four-person apartments across from the pharmacy overlooking the main street (and beyond the train noise). One has a terrace and fridge (top floor); the other has windows and a full kitchen (Db-€95, Tb-€115, Qb-€130, prices include city tax, cash only, reception just before the tobacco shop near Piazza Marconi at Via Visconti 10, tel. 0187-821-181, mobile 340-267-5009, www.rosacamere.it, rosa.vitali@libero.it).

$$ Francamaria and her husband Andrea rent 10 sharp, comfortable, and creatively renovated rooms—all described in detail on her website. While their reception desk is on the harbor square (on the ground floor facing the harbor at Piazza Marconi 30—don't confuse it with Albergo Barbara at same address), the rooms they manage are all over town (Db-€95-145 depending on size and view, Qb-€130-160, extra person-€20, cash only, some with air-con, Wi-Fi is spotty, tel. 0187-812-002, mobile 328-711-9728, www.francamaria.com, info@francamaria.com).

More Private Rooms in Vernazza

Rooms from Emanuela Colombo, Maria Capellini, and Manuela Moggia are not located on the map in this chapter; arrange a meeting time and/or ask for directions when you reserve.

$$ Vernazza Rooms, run by Daria Bianchi, Chiara, and Davide, rents 11 decent rooms: Four are above the Blue Marlin Bar looking down on the main street, and seven are a steep climb higher up, just under the city hall (Db-€85-100, Tb-€100, Qb-€120-140; price depends on view, location, and size; ring bell at Via Roma 41—next to Blue Marlin Bar, a few with air-con and others with fans, very limited English spoken, mobile 338-581-4688 or 338-413-8696, www.vernazzarooms.com, info@vernazzarooms.com).

$$ Emanuela Colombo has two rooms—one spacious and classy on the harbor square (Db-€95), the other a *molto* chic split-level apartment located on a quiet side street (Db-€100, Qb-€140; tel. 339-834-2486, www.vacanzemanuela.it, manucap64@libero.it).

$$ Rooms Francesca's two tidy rooms and one apartment hide out in the steep streets just below city hall (non-view Db-€70, seaview Db-€85, 2-room apartment: Db-€90/Qb-€130; check in

at Enoteca Sciacchetrà at Via Roma 19, tel. 0187-821-112, www.
5terre-vernazza.it, moggia.franco@libero.it, Francesca and Franco).

$$ Ivo's Camere rents two simple no-terrace rooms high
above the main street (Db-€80, air-con, Via Roma 6, reception at
Pizzeria Fratelli Basso—Via Roma 1, mobile 333-477-5521, www.
ivocamere.com, post@ivocamere.com).

$$ Maria Capellini rents a couple of simple, clean rooms,
including one on the ground floor right on the harbor (Db with
kitchen-€95, Tb-€120, cash only, fans, mobile 338-436-3411,
www.mariacapellini.com, mariacapellini@hotmail.it, kindly Maria
and Giacomo).

More Options: **$$ Rooms Elisabetta** (3 tight, recently reno-
vated, casually run rooms at the tip-top of town with Vernazza's ul-
timate 360-degree roof terrace—come here for the views, Db-€80,
Tb-€100, Qb-€110, these prices if you book direct and pay cash,
fans, partway up Corniglia path at Via Carattino 62, mobile 347-
451-1834, www.elisabettacarro.it, carroelisabetta@hotmail.com,
Elisabetta); **$$ Capitano Rooms** (3 recently remodeled rooms several flights of stairs above main drag, Db-€90, includes breakfast,
fans; ask for Julia, Paolo, or Barbara at Trattoria del Capitano restaurant on main square at Piazza Marconi 21; tel. 0187-812-201,
www.tavernavernazza.com, info@tavernavernazza.com); **$$ Eva's
Rooms** (3 rooms overlooking main street, Sb-€50, D with private
bath outside the room-€90, Db-€100, air-con, train noise, meet
at boutique at Via Roma 68, tel. 334-798-6500, www.evasrooms.
it, evasrooms@yahoo.it); and **$$ Manuela Moggia** (5 rooms, Db-
€80, Db with kitchen or view-€120, Tb-€95, Tb with kitchen or
view-€130, Qb with kitchen-€145, some behind train station at
Via Gavino 22, tel. 0187-812-397, mobile 333-413-6374, www.
manuela-vernazza.com, info@manuela-vernazza.com).

Eating in Vernazza

BREAKFAST

Locals take breakfast about as seriously as flossing. A cappuccino
and a pastry or a piece of focaccia from a bar or bakery does it. Most
of my recommended accommodations don't come with breakfast
(when they do, I've noted so in my listings). Assuming you're on
your own, you have five basic options: Blue Marlin Bar and Del
Capitano for their extensive menus; Il Pirata delle Cinque Terre
for sugary stuff and a lively welcome; Ananasso Bar for coffee and
a sweet roll on the harborfront; or any bakery for picnic goodies.

Blue Marlin Bar (midtown, just below the train station)
serves a good array of clearly priced à la carte items including eggs
and bacon (only after 8:30), likely to total €10 with a *caffè lungo*. It's
run by Massimo and Carmen with the capable assistance of Jeff, an

American who now lives in Vernazza. If you're awaiting a train any time of day, the Blue Marlin's outdoor seating beats the platform (Thu-Tue 7:00-24:00, closed Wed).

Trattoria del Capitano offers outdoor seating on the harbor, as well as cozy spots inside the restaurant. You can order single items (€6 egg dishes including focaccia and small salad) or opt for the €12 full-and-filling breakfast (Wed-Mon from 8:00, closed Tue except in Aug).

Il Pirata delle Cinque Terre, an endearing tourist trap, is located in the workaday zone at the parking lot at the top of town. The dynamic Sicilian duo Gianluca and Massimo (hardworking twins, a.k.a. the Cannoli brothers) enthusiastically offer a wide assortment of Sicilian pastries. Their fun, playful service makes up for the lack of a view. Massimo is a likeable loudmouth, while Gianluca is a pastry artist. Posted on the wall by the door is their clear and concise breakfast list in English, with prices divided between sweet and savory. Their sweet pastry breakfasts include an array of treats like *panzerotto* (made of ricotta, cinnamon, and vanilla, €2.50) and hot cheese and pesto bruschetta (€3). They proudly serve no bacon and eggs (since "this is Italy"). While the atmosphere of the place seems like suburban Milan, it has a curious charisma among its customers (daily 6:30-24:00, Via Gavino 36, tel. 0187-812-047).

Ananasso Bar feels Old World, with youthful energy and a great location with little tables right on the harbor. They offer toasted *panini,* pastries, and designer cappuccino. You can eat a bit cheaper at the bar (you're welcome to picnic on the nearby bench or seawall rocks with a Mediterranean view) or enjoy the best-situated tables in town (Fri-Wed 8:00-late, closed Thu).

Picnic Breakfast: Drop by one of Vernazza's several little bakeries, focaccia shops, or grocery stores to assemble a breakfast to eat on the breakwater. Top it off with a coffee in a nearby bar.

LUNCH AND DINNER

If you enjoy Italian cuisine and seafood, Vernazza's restaurants are worth the splurge. All take pride in their cooking. Wander around at about 20:00 and compare the ambience, but don't wait too late to eat—many kitchens close at 22:00. (Immigrants, who are doing more and more of the hard work of cooking and cleaning, need to wrap things up in time to catch the last train back to La Spezia, where many of them live.) If you dine in Vernazza but are staying in another town, be sure to check train schedules before sitting down to eat, as trains run less frequently in the evening (with a nearly 2-hour wait after the 21:30 departure). To get an outdoor table on summer weekends, reserve ahead. Expect to spend around

Monterosso al Mare (Town #5)

This is a resort with a few cars and lots of hotels, rentable beach umbrellas, crowds, and a little more late-night action than the neighboring towns. Monterosso al Mare—the only Cinque Terre  town built on flat land—has two parts: A new town (called Fegina) with a parking lot, train station, and TI; and an old town (Centro Storico), which cradles Old World charm in its small, crooked lanes. In the old town, you'll find hole-in-the-wall shops, pastel townscapes, and a new generation of creative small-businesspeople eager to keep their visitors happy.

A pedestrian tunnel connects the old with the new, but take a small detour around the point for a nicer walk. It offers a close-up view of two sights: a 16th-century lookout tower, built after the last serious pirate raid in 1545; and a Nazi "pillbox," a small, low concrete bunker where gunners hid. (During World War II, nearby La Spezia was an important Axis naval base, and Monterosso was bombed while the Germans were here.)

Strolling the waterfront promenade, you can pick out each of the Cinque Terre towns decorating the coast. After dark, they sparkle. Monterosso is the most enjoyable of the five for young travelers wanting to connect with others looking for a little evening action. Even so, Monterosso is not a full-blown Portofino-style resort—and locals appreciate quiet, sensitive guests.

Monterosso sustained serious damage in the 2011 flood, but within just a few months, it was back up and running at nearly 100 percent. Walking through the town today, you'll have to know where to look to find evidence of the devastation. Big grates on the six roads cover the historic canals (which drain runoff from the surrounding hills into the sea), and the sound of rushing water reassures townsfolk that the streams are flowing unimpeded below.

Orientation to Monterosso

TOURIST INFORMATION

The TI Proloco is next to the train station (April-Oct daily 9:00-19:00, closed Nov-March, exit station and go left a few doors, tel. 0187-817-506, www.prolocomonterosso.it). For national park tickets and information, head upstairs within the station to the ticket office near platform 1 (likely daily 8:00-20:00, shorter hours

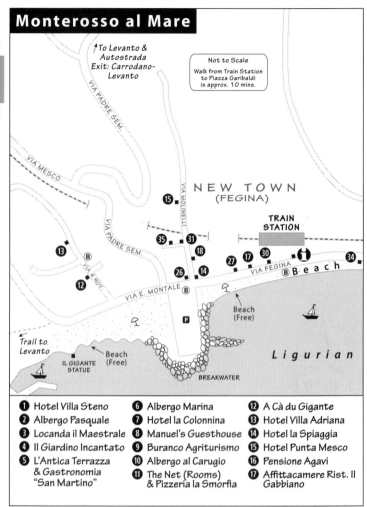

Monterosso al Mare

To Levanto &
Autostrada
Exit: Carrodano-
Levanto

Not to Scale

Walk from Train Station
to Piazza Garibaldi
is approx. 10 mins.

VIA PADRE SEM.

VIA MESCO

VIA PADRE SEM.

VIA MOLINELLI

N E W   T O W N
(FEGINA)

TRAIN
STATION

❶ **15**

13

Ⓑ

VIA 4 NOV.

12

VIA E. MONTALE

35 **31**

18

26 **14**

Ⓑ

27 **17** **30**

Ⓑ

ⓘ

VIA FEGINA   **34**

B e a c h

Beach
(Free)

Ⓟ

Trail to
Levanto

IL GIGANTE
STATUE

Beach
(Free)

BREAKWATER

L i g u r i a n

❶ Hotel Villa Steno	❻ Albergo Marina	⓬ A Cà du Gigante
❷ Albergo Pasquale	❼ Hotel la Colonnina	⓭ Hotel Villa Adriana
❸ Locanda il Maestrale	❽ Manuel's Guesthouse	⓮ Hotel la Spiaggia
❹ Il Giardino Incantato	❾ Buranco Agriturismo	⓯ Hotel Punta Mesco
❺ L'Antica Terrazza & Gastronomia "San Martino"	❿ Albergo al Carugio	⓰ Pensione Agavi
	⓫ The Net (Rooms) & Pizzeria la Smorfia	⓱ Affittacamere Rist. Il Gabbiano

off-season). If you arrive late on a summer day, the old town's Internet café is helpful with tourist information (see later).

Rebuild Monterosso: Led by a group of American women who married into the community, Rebuild Monterosso brought relief to the town in the immediate aftermath of the flood and has since evolved into an organization focused on fostering healthy tourism and keeping visitors up-to-date on the latest in town (www.facebook.com/WeCanRebuildMonterosso).

ARRIVAL IN MONTEROSSO

By Train: Train travelers arrive in the new town, from which it's a scenic, flat 10-minute stroll to all the old town action (leave station

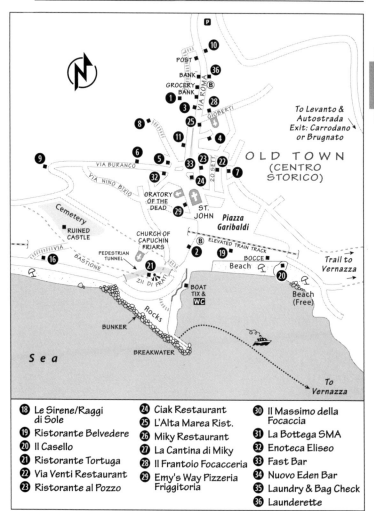

18 Le Sirene/Raggi di Sole	**24** Ciak Restaurant	**30** Il Massimo della Focaccia
19 Ristorante Belvedere	**25** L'Alta Marea Rist.	**31** La Bottega SMA
20 Il Casello	**26** Miky Restaurant	**32** Enoteca Eliseo
21 Ristorante Tortuga	**27** La Cantina di Miky	**33** Fast Bar
22 Via Venti Restaurant	**28** Il Frantoio Focacceria	**34** Nuovo Eden Bar
23 Ristorante al Pozzo	**29** Emy's Way Pizzeria Friggitoria	**35** Laundry & Bag Check
		36 Launderette

to the left; to reach hotels in the new town, turn right out of station). The bar at track 1, which overlooks both the tracks and the beach, is a handy place to hang out while waiting for your train to pull in (salads, sandwiches, drinks). As many trains run late, this can turn a frustration into a blessing.

Shuttle buses run along the waterfront between the old town (Piazza Garibaldi, just beyond the tunnel), the train station, and the parking lot at the end of Via Fegina (*Campo Sportivo* stop). The bus saves you a 10-minute schlep with your bags but only goes once an hour, and is likely not worth the trouble (€1.50 one-way, €2.50 on board, free with Cinque Terre park card).

The other alternative is to take a **taxi** (certain vehicles have

CINQUE TERRE

permission to drive in the old city center). They usually wait outside the train station, but you may have to call (€7 from station to the old town, mobile 335-616-5842, 335-616-5845, or 335-628-0933).

By Car: Monterosso is 30 minutes off the freeway (exit: Carrodano-Levanto). Note that about three miles above Monterosso, there's an intersection that causes most drivers an unnecessary and time-consuming mistake: A poorly signed fork directs you to either *Monterosso Centro Storico* (old part of town—Via Roma parking lot with only a few spots, and the new Loreto garage) or *Fegina* (the new town and beachfront parking, most likely where you want to go). At this point you must choose your destination, because you can't drive directly from the new town to the old center (which is closed to cars without special permits).

Most people driving into Monterosso should choose the *Fegina* fork. Parking is easy (except July-Aug and summer weekends) in the huge beachfront guarded lot in the new town (€18/24 hours).

If instead you head to the old town, you'll find the Loreto parking garage on Via Roma, a 10-minute downhill walk to the main square (€1.70/hour, €18/24 hours). For the cheapest Monterosso rates, park along the blue lines (€8/day, a few minutes farther uphill from the Loreto garage).

See "Cinque Terre Connections" at the end of this chapter for directions from Milan and tips on driving in the Cinque Terre.

HELPFUL HINTS

Medical Help: The town's bike-riding, leather bag-toting, English-speaking physician is **Dr. Vitone,** who charges €50-80 for a simple visit (less for poor students, mobile 338-853-0949, vitonee@yahoo.it).

Thursday Morning Market: Every Thursday morning, trucks pull into the old town and fill the public area by the beach with temporary stalls where locals get the items not otherwise available in this small town.

Internet Access: The Net, a few steps off the old town's main drag (Via Roma), has high-speed computers and Wi-Fi (under €1/10 minutes). Enzo happily provides information on the Cinque Terre, rents rooms (see "Sleeping in Monterosso," later), and sells power adapters and memory cards (daily 9:30-23:00, off-season until 19:00, Via Vittorio Emanuele 55, tel. 0187-817-288, www.monterossonet.com, info@monterossonet.com).

Baggage Storage: Wash and Dry Lavarapido, two blocks from the station, provides a wonderful €5 bag-check service (details in next listing).

Laundry: For full-service laundry in the new town, drop off your laundry in the morning at **Wash and Dry Lavarapido** and have it returned to your hotel by evening—or have them do a pick-up/drop-off for the same price. Since the owners speak Italian only, have your hotelier arrange the details (€13/load, daily 8:00-19:00, Via Molinelli 17, mobile 339-484-0940, Lucia and Ivano). If you'd rather wash your own clothes, head to the **Luètu Lavanderia** in the old town, uphill on Via Roma, across from the post office (€4/wash, €1/dry—12 minutes, €1 detergent, daily 8:00-22:00, tel. 328-286-1908).

Boat Trips: Stefano or **Nico** can take you on a cruise around the Cinque Terre (€100/hour, one hour is enough for a quick spin, two hours includes time for swimming stops; longer trips to Portovenere and offshore islands also possible). Stefano's boat, *Matilde,* holds up to six people, while Nico's boat takes up to four and is slightly cheaper (about €50 one-way to Vernazza, €80 one-way to Riomaggiore, €300 to Portovenere; Stefano's mobile 333-821-2007, Nico's mobile 339-564-0907, www.matildenavigazione.com, info@matildenavigazione.com).

Massage: Giorgio Moggia, the local physiotherapist, gives good massages at your hotel or in his studio (€65/hour, tel. 339-314-6127, giomogg@tin.it).

Monterosso Walk

This self-guided walk will introduce you to Monterosso, beginning with an easy and lazy sweep of the head from the breakwater. Part 1, focusing on the mostly level town center, takes about 30 minutes; for Part 2, summiting the adjacent hill, allow another hour or so.

Part 1: Monterosso Harbor and Town Center

• *Hike out from the dock in the old town and climb five rough steps to the very top of the concrete...*

Breakwater: If you're visiting by boat, you'll start here anyway. From this point you can survey Monterosso's old town (straight ahead) and new town (stretching to the left, with train station and parking lot). Notice the bluff that separates old and new, and imagine how much harder your commute would be if the narrow road tethering these two towns were somehow cut off. It happened in the spring of 2013, when the wall below the Capuchin church (at the top of the hill) gave way, creating a landslide. For a time, the only ways to connect the two halves of town were to drive six miles around...or hike up and over this hill. (The little fort halfway up the hill, which dates from 1550, is now a private home.)

Looking to the right, you can actually see all *cinque* of the *terre* from one spot: Vernazza, Corniglia (above the shore), Manarola, and a few buildings of Riomaggiore beyond that.

These days, the harbor hosts more paddleboats than fishing boats. Sand erosion is a major problem. The partial breakwater (a row of giant rocks in the middle of the harbor) is designed to save the beach from washing away. While old-timers remember a vast beach, their grandchildren truck in sand each spring to give tourists something to lie on. (The Nazis liked the Cinque Terre, too—find two of their bomb-hardened bunkers, near left and far right.)

The fancy €300-a-night, four-star Hotel Porto Roca (pink building high on the hill, on the far right of the harbor) marks the trail to Vernazza. High above, you see an example of the costly roads built in the 1980s to connect the Cinque Terre towns with the freeway over the hills.

The two prominent capes (Punta di Montenero to the right, and Punta Mesco to the left) define the Cinque Terre region. The closer cape, Punta Mesco, marks an important sea-life sanctuary, home to a rare sea grass that provides an ideal home for fish eggs. Buoys keep fishing boats away. The cape was once a quarry, providing employment to locals who chipped out the stones used to build the local towns (the greenish stones making up part of the breakwater below you are from there).

On the far end of the new town, marking the best free beach around, you can just see the statue named *Il Gigante* (hard to spot because it blends in with the gray rock). It's 45 feet tall and once held a trident. While it looks as if it were hewn from the rocky cliff, it's actually made of reinforced concrete and dates from the beginning of the 20th century, when it supported a dancing terrace for a *fin de siècle* villa. A violent storm left the giant holding nothing but memories of Monterosso's glamorous age.

• *From the breakwater, walk into the old town. At the top of the beach, notice the openings of two big drains, ready to let flash floods rip through town without destroying things. Walking under the train tracks, venture right into the square and find the statue of a dandy holding what looks like a box cutter.*

Piazza Garibaldi: The statue honors Giuseppe Garibaldi, the dashing firebrand revolutionary who, in the 1860s, helped unite the people of Italy into a modern nation. Facing Garibaldi, with your back to the sea, you'll see (from right to left) the orange city hall (with the now-required European Union flag beside the Italian one) and a big home and recreation center for poor and homeless elderly. You'll also see A Ca' du Sciensa restaurant (with historic town photos inside and upstairs; you're welcome to pop in for a look).

After the 2011 flood, it was on this square that the National Guard set up an emergency tent, used for staging emergency deliveries, community meals, Christmas Eve Mass, and the New Year's Eve disco. In the aftermath of the flood, many moving stories emerged. Old ladies who couldn't help dig, helped cook. People worried that Laura, whose bakery—loved for her secret recipes—

grappa menu. The seating is in three zones: overlooking the beach, in the garden, or in the cellar. Run by Manuel, son of well-known local restaurateur Miky, it sometimes hosts live music. Manuel offers a fun "five villages" wine tasting with local meats and cheeses (€15/person for just wine, €20/person with food). Microbrews are becoming popular in Italy, and this is the best place in town for top-end Italian beers (Thu-Tue until late, closed Wed, Via Fegina 90, tel. 0187-802-525).

Nuovo Eden Bar, overlooking the beach by the big rock just east of the train station, is a fine place to enjoy a cocktail or fancy ice cream with a sea view. During happy hour (17:00-19:00), €6 cocktails come with a snack. Locals consider their ice cream (either to-go from the streetside stand, or fancy and sit-down) the best in town. Consider this place for a pre-dinner drink or dessert with a view (daily 7:30-24:00, closed Mon off-season).

Sleeping in Monterosso

Monterosso, the most beach-resorty of the five Cinque Terre towns, offers maximum comfort and ease. The TI Proloco just outside the train station can give you a list of €70-80 double rooms. Rooms in Monterosso are a better value for your money than similar rooms in crowded Vernazza, and the proprietors seem more genuine and welcoming.

IN THE OLD TOWN

$$$ Hotel Villa Steno is lovingly managed and features great view balconies, panoramic gardens and a roof terrace with sun beds, air-conditioning, and the friendly help of English-speaking Matteo and his wife, Carla. Of their 16 rooms, 14 have view balconies (Sb-€120, Db-€190, Tb-€230, Qb-€265, includes hearty buffet breakfast, €10/night discount in 2016 when you pay cash and show this book, laundry, parking-€10—reserve in advance, hike up to the panoramic terrace, Via Roma 109, tel. 0187-817-028 or 0187-818-336, www.villasteno.com, steno@pasini.com). It's a 15-minute hike (or €8 taxi ride) from the train station to the top of the old town. Readers get a free Cinque Terre info packet and a glass of local wine when they check in—ask for it.

$$$ Albergo Pasquale is a modern, comfortable place with 15 seaview rooms, run by the same family as the Hotel Villa Steno (above). It's conveniently located just a few steps from the beach, boat dock, tunnel entrance to the new town, and train tracks. While there is some train noise, the soundtrack is mostly a lullaby of waves. Located right on the harbor, it has an elevator and offers easier access than most (same prices and welcome drink as Villa Steno; air-con, laundry service, Via Fegina 8, tel. 0187-817-550 or 0187-817-477, www.hotelpasquale.it, pasquale@pasini.com, Felicita and Marco).

$$$ Locanda il Maestrale rents six small, stylish rooms in a sophisticated and peaceful little inn. Although renovated with all the modern comforts, it retains centuries-old character under frescoed ceilings. Its peaceful sun terrace overlooking the old town and Via Roma action is a delight (small Db-€115, Db-€150, superior Db-€180, prices lower off-season, 10 percent Rick Steves discount in 2016 if you book directly with hotel and pay cash, air-con, Via Roma 37, tel. 0187-817-013, mobile 338-4530-531, www.locandamaestrale.net, maestrale@monterossonet.com, Stefania).

$$$ Il Giardino Incantato ("The Enchanted Garden") is a charming and comfortable four-room B&B with impressive attention to detail in a tastefully renovated 16th-century Ligurian home in the heart of the old town. Sip their homemade *limoncino* upon check-in and have breakfast under lemon trees in a delightful hidden garden, which is illuminated with candles in the evening (Db-€150-170, Db suite-€180-200, ask for Rick Steves discount when you pay in cash, air-con, free minibar and tea and coffee service, laundry service-€15/load, Via Mazzini 18, tel. 0187-818-315, mobile 333-264-9252, www.ilgiardinoincantato.net, giardino_incantato@libero.it, kind and eager-to-please Fausto and Mariapia).

$$$ L'Antica Terrazza rents four classy rooms right in town. With a pretty terrace overlooking the pedestrian street and minimal stairs, Raffaella and John offer a good deal (D with private bath down the hall-€85, Db-€115, these special prices for Rick Steves readers, €5 discount when you pay in cash, air-con, Vicolo San Martino 1, mobile 380-138-0082 or 347-132-6213, www.anticaterrazza.com, post@anticaterrazza.com).

$$$ Albergo Marina, creatively run by enthusiastic husband-and-wife team Marina and Eraldo, has 23 decent rooms and a garden with lemon trees. With a free and filling buffet featuring local specialties from 14:00 to 17:00 daily, they offer a fine value (Db-€150, Tb-€175, Qb-€200, 15 percent discount in 2016 when you pay in cash and show this book, elevator, air-con, free use of kayak and snorkel equipment, Via Buranco 40, tel. 0187-817-613, www.hotelmarina5terre.com, marina@hotelmarina5terre.com).

$$$ Hotel la Colonnina has 21 big rooms (some older, some stylishly up-to-date), generous if dated public spaces, and several leafy, peaceful sun terraces. It's buried in the town's fragrant and sleepy back streets (Db-€158, Tb-€198, Qb-€248, €5 more for non-view mini-terrace, €15 more for townview terrace, cash only, air-con, fridges, elevator, inviting rooftop terrace with sun beds, garden, in the old town a block inland from the main square at Via Zuecca 6, tel. 0187-817-439, www.lacolonninacinqueterre.it, info@lacolonninacinqueterre.it, Cristina).

$$$ Manuel's Guesthouse, perched high above the town among terraces, is a garden getaway run by Lorenzo and his father, Giovanni (and named for their uncle/brother, a disheveled artist who prefers to set up his easels down below these days). They have six big, bright rooms and a grand view. After climbing the killer stairs from the town center, their killer terrace is hard to leave—especially after a few drinks (Db-€130, big Db with grand-view balcony-€140, cash only, air-con, up about 100 steps behind church—you can ask Lorenzo to carry your bags up the hill, Via San Martino 39, mobile 333-439-0809, www.manuelsguesthouse. com, manuelsguesthouse@libero.it).

$$$ Buranco Agriturismo, a 10-minute hike above the old town, has wonderful gardens and views over the vine-covered valley. Its primary business is wine and olive-oil production, but they offer three apartments at a good price. It's a rare opportunity to stay in a farmhouse but still be able to get to town on foot (2-6 people-€60/person including breakfast, €30/child under 10, air-con, €10 taxi from station, tel. 0187-817-677, mobile 349-434-8046, www.burancocinqueterre.it, info@buranco.it, informally run by Loredana, Mary, and Giulietta).

$$ Albergo al Carugio is a simple, practical nine-room place in a big apartment-style building at the top of the old town. It's quiet, comfy, and functional (Db-€85, this price for Rick Steves readers who book direct and pay cash, no breakfast, air-con, Via Roma 100, tel. 0187-817-453, www.alcarugio.it, info@alcarugio. it, Andrea and Simona).

$$ The Net Room Service is run by Enzo, who owns the Internet point in town (and speaks perfect English). Offering Monterosso's least expensive accommodations, he manages a dozen or so apartments, most in the old town and a few in the new town away from the train noise. Enzo's office functions as your reception (Db-€60-80, Qb-€120-150, prices based on size and view, 2- or 3-night minimum stay, Via Vittorio Emanuele 55, tel. 0187-817-288, mobile 335-778-5085, www.monterossonet.com, info@monterossonet.com).

IN THE NEW TOWN

$$$ A Cà du Gigante, despite its name, is a tiny yet stylish refuge with nine rooms. About 100 yards from the beach (and surrounded by blocky apartments on a modern street), the interior is tastefully done with modern comfort in mind (Db-€160, Db seaview suite-€180, 10 percent discount with 3-night stay and this book in 2016, occasional last-minute deals, air-con, free parking, Via IV Novembre 11, tel. 0187-817-401, www.ilgigantecinqueterre.it, gigante@ilgigantecinqueterre.it, Claudia).

$$$ Hotel Villa Adriana is a big, contemporary, bright hotel on a church-owned estate set in a peaceful garden with a pool, free parking, and a no-stress style. They rent 54 rooms—some with terraces and/or sea views—at the same price as much simpler places on the water (Sb-€95, Db-€175, all with showers, air-con, elevator, free loaner bikes, Via IV Novembre 23, tel. 0187-818-109, www.villaadriana.info, info@villaadriana.info).

$$$ Hotel la Spiaggia is a venerable old 19-room place facing the beach and run with attitude by Andrea Poggi and his gentle daughter Maria. Half of the rooms come with sea views (Db-€170, view Db-€180, extra bed-€30, free parking, cash only, air-con, elevator, Via Lungomare 96, tel. 0187-817-567, www.laspiaggiahotel.com, hotellaspiaggia@libero.it).

$$$ Hotel Punta Mesco is a tidy, well-run little haven renting 17 quiet, casual rooms. While none have views, 10 rooms have small terraces. For the price, it may offer the best comfort in town (Db-€153, Tb-€185, €10 discount off these prices with cash, air-con, parking, Via Molinelli 35, tel. 0187-817-495, www.hotelpuntamesco.it, info@hotelpuntamesco.it, Diego, Karina, Manuel, and Roberto).

$$$ Pensione Agavi has 10 spartan, bright, overpriced rooms, about half overlooking the beach near the big rock. This is not a place to party—it feels like an old hospital with narrow hallways (D-€90, Db-€120, Tb-€145, 10 percent discount for 3 nights or more, breakfast-€15, cash only, refrigerators, turn left out of station to Fegina 30, tel. 0187-817-171, mobile 333-697-4071, www.hotelagavi.com, info@hotelagavi.com, Hillary).

$$ Affittacamere Ristorante il Gabbiano is a touristy restaurant right on the beach, renting five quiet, air-conditioned rooms upstairs. Three rooms face the sea, with small balconies (Db-€110, the largest can be Tb-€130, Qb-€160), while two are at the back, facing a little garden (Db-€100). The Gabbiano family restaurant serves as your reception (cash only, air-con, Via Fegina 84, tel. 0187-817-578, www.affittacamereristoranteilgabbiano.com, affittacamereilgabbiano@live.it).

$ Le Sirene/Raggi di Sole, with nine simple rooms in two humble buildings, is about the cheapest place in town. It's run from a hole-in-the-wall reception desk a block from the station, just off the water. I'd request the Le Sirene building, which doesn't have train noise and is a bit more spacious and airy than Raggi di Sole (Sb-€70, Db-€90, third person-€30, 10 percent discount in 2016 with this book, fans, Via Molinelli 10, mobile 331-788-1088, www.sirenerooms.com, sirenerooms@gmail.com, Ermanna).

Eating in Monterosso

WITH A SEA VIEW

Of these seaview restaurants, the first two offer reasonable prices right on the old town beach, while the last is a romantic splurge higher up.

Ristorante Belvedere, big and sprawling, is *the* place for a good-value meal indoors or outdoors on the harborfront. Their *anfora belvedere*—mixed seafood stew dumped dramatically at the table from a pottery amphora into your bowl—is huge, and can easily be split among up to four diners (€48). Share with your group and add pasta for a fine meal. Mussel fans will enjoy the *tagliolini della casa* (€9). Their *misto mare* plate (2-person minimum, €15/person), a fishy treat, can nearly make an entire meal. It's energetically run by Federico and Roberto (€8-10 pastas, €10-19 *secondi,* Wed-Mon 12:00-14:30 & 18:00-22:00, closed Tue except Aug, on the harbor in the old town, tel. 0187-817-033).

Il Casello is the only place for a fun meal on a terrace overlooking the old town beach. With outdoor tables on a rocky outcrop, it's a pleasant spot for a salad, pasta, or *secondi* (€9-13 pastas, €14-18 *secondi,* daily April-Oct 12:00-22:00, closed Nov-March, mobile 333-492-7629, Bacco).

Ristorante Tortuga is the top option in Monterosso for seaview elegance, with gorgeous outdoor seating high on a bluff and a lovely white-tablecloth-and-candles interior. If you're looking for a place to propose, this offers the prettiest and most romantic dining in town. When you're out and about, drop by to consider which table you'd like to reserve for later. House specialties include *cannelloni tortuga* (stuffed not with turtle, but with sea bass) and *filetto Sciacchetrà*—steak with a glaze made of the local sweet wine (€14-19 pastas, €15-20 *secondi,* Tue-Sun 12:00-15:00 & 18:00-22:00, closed Mon, just outside the tunnel that connects the old and new town—or climb up the ramp in front of Albergo Pasquale, tel. 0187-800-065, mobile 333-240-7956, Silvia and Giamba).

IN THE OLD TOWN

Via Venti is a quiet little trattoria, hidden in an alley deep in the heart of the old town, where Papa Ettore and co-chef Ilaria create imaginative seafood dishes using the day's catch and freshly made pasta. Ilaria's husband Michele serves up delicate and savory gnocchi (tiny potato dumplings) with crab sauce, tender ravioli stuffed with fresh fish, and pear-and-pecorino pasta. There's nothing pretentious here...just good cooking, service, and prices (€13-14 pastas, €16-20 *secondi,* Fri-Wed 12:00-14:30 & 18:30-22:30, closed Thu, Via XX Settembre 32, tel. 0187-818-347).

Ristorante al Pozzo is a favorite among locals. It's family-run, with good old-fashioned quality, as Gino (with his long white beard) cooks, and his engaging English-speaking son, Manuel, serves. They have one of the best wine lists in town, serve only homemade pasta, and are known for their raw fish and wonderful seafood *antipasti misti* (€10-16 pastas, €15-25 *secondi*, Fri-Wed 12:00-15:00 & 18:30-22:30, closed Thu, Via Roma 24, tel. 0187-817-575).

Ciak, high-energy and tightly packed, is a local institution with reliably good food and higher prices. It's known for its huge, sizzling terra-cotta crock for two crammed with the day's catch and accompanied by risotto or spaghetti, or served swimming in a soup *(zuppa).* Other popular choices are fish ravioli with shrimp sauce and the seafood *antipasto Lampara* (€20). Stroll a couple of paces past the outdoor tables up Via Roma to see what Signore Ciak (who wears his Popeye cap in the kitchen) has on the stove. Reservations are smart in summer (€12-14 pastas, €18-20 *secondi,* Thu-Tue 12:00-15:00 & 18:00-22:30, closed Wed, Piazza Don Minzoni 6, tel. 0187-817-014, www.ristoranteciak.net).

L'Alta Marea offers special fish ravioli, the catch of the day, and huge crocks of fresh, steamed mussels. Young chef Marco cooks with charisma, while his wife, Anna, takes good care of the guests. This place is quieter, buried in the old town two blocks off the beach, and has covered tables out front for people-watching (€10-13 pastas and pizza, €15-17 *secondi,* 10 percent discount in 2016 with cash and this book, Thu-Tue 12:00-15:00 & 18:00-22:00, closed Wed, Via Roma 54, tel. 0187-817-170).

Gastronomia "San Martino," warmly and passionately run by Moreno, is a tiny, humble place with almost no ambience (except for a couple of outdoor tables) that serves inexpensive quality dishes on plastic plates. Eat inside, outside, or take away. Order from the daily menu on the blackboard (€6 pastas, €10 *secondi,* Tue-Sun 12:00-15:00 & 18:00-22:00, closed Mon, next to recommended L'Antica Terrazza hotel at Vicolo San Martino 2, mobile 346-109-7338).

IN THE NEW TOWN

Even if you're not sleeping in the new town, consider venturing over for dinner at one of these options; as a bonus, the walk is mostly along a scenic and lively beachfront promenade.

Miky is packed with well-dressed locals who know their seafood and want to eat it in a classy environment. For elegantly presented, top-quality food, with subtle flavors that celebrate local ingredients and traditions, this is my Cinque Terre favorite. It's clearly a proud family operation: Miky (dad), Simonetta (mom), charming Sara (daughter, who greets guests), and the attentive but easygoing waitstaff all work hard. All their pasta is "pizza pasta"—cooked normally but finished in a bowl that's encased in a thin pizza crust. They cook the concoction in a wood-fired oven to keep in the aroma, then flambé it at your table. Miky's has a fine wine list with many available by the glass if you ask. If I were ever to require a dessert, it would be their mixed sampler plate, *dolce misto*—€10 and plenty for two (€13-21 fun-to-share *antipasti*, €17-18 pastas, €18-30 *secondi*, €8 sweets, Wed-Mon 12:00-15:00 & 19:00-23:00, closed Tue, reservations wise in summer, diners tend to dress up a bit—but it's not required, in the new town 100 yards from train station at Via Fegina 104, tel. 0187-817-608, www.ristorantemiky.it).

La Cantina di Miky, a few doors down (toward the station), serves Ligurian specialties that follow in Miky's family tradition of quality. Run by son Manuel—and Christine from New Jersey—it's more trendy, youthful, and informal than Miky's. You can sit downstairs, in the garden, or overlooking the sea (€18 anchovy tasting plate, €10-13 pastas, €14-18 *secondi,* creative desserts, large selection of Italian microbrews, Thu-Tue 12:00-24:00, closed Wed, Via Fegina 90, tel. 0187-802-525). This place doubles as a cocktail bar in the evenings—see "Nightlife in Monterosso," earlier.

LIGHT MEALS, TAKEOUT FOOD, AND BREAKFAST

In the Old Town: Lots of shops and bakeries sell pizza and focaccia for an easy picnic at the beach or on the trail. **Pizzeria la Smorfia**—the local favorite for pizza—cooks up good pizza to eat in or take out. Pizzas come in two sizes; the large can feed three (small pizzas-€6-8, large pizzas-€14-19, Fri-Wed 11:00-24:00, Via Vittorio Emanuele 73, tel. 0187-818-395). At **Il Frantoio,** Simone makes tasty pizza and focaccia to go or to munch perched on a stool (Fri-Wed 9:00-13:45 & 16:30-19:30, closed Thu, just off Via Roma at Via Gioberti 1). **Emy's Way Pizzeria Friggitoria** offers thick-crust pizzas—whole and by the slice—for casual seating or takeout. Emy also serves up deep-fried seafood in to-go cones (€5-9 pizza, €3-7 *fritti,* daily 11:00-20:00, later in summer, along the skinny street next to the church, Emiliano).

In the New Town, near the Station: For a quick bite right at the train station (or on the beach), consider **Il Massimo della Focaccia.** Massimo and Daniella serve local quiche-like tortes, sandwiches, focaccia pizzas, and desserts. With benches just in front, this is a good bet for a €3-4 light meal with a sea view (Thu-Tue 9:00-19:00, closed Wed except June-Aug, Via Fegina 50 at the entry to the station). **La Bottega SMA** is a smart minimart with fresh produce, *antipasti,* deli items, and other picnic fare. They'll even make you a sandwich: Select a bread and filling, and pay by weight (daily 8:00-13:00 & 16:30-19:30 except Wed and Sun until 13:00, near Lavarapido at Vittoria Gianni 21).

Breakfast: Most hotels include breakfast in the room rate. But if you're out looking for breakfast, in the new town, consider **Bar Gio,** near the train station on the waterfront (continental breakfasts) or **Wine & Food,** with €5 egg dishes and a €10 "American Breakfast" (Via Vittorio Emanuele 26); in the old town, look for **Bar Davi,** under the arch on Via Roma in the old town (with an American-style option, daily 7:00 until late, may close Wed, Guido).

Cinque Terre Connections

BY TRAIN

The five towns of the Cinque Terre are on a pokey milk-run train line. Erratically timed but roughly hourly trains connect each town with the others, plus La Spezia, Genoa, and Riviera towns to the north. While a few of these local trains go to more distant points (Milan or Pisa), it's much faster to change in La Spezia, Monterosso, or Sestri Levante to a bigger train (local train info tel. 0187-817-458, www.trenitalia.com).

From La Spezia Centrale by Train to: Rome (8/day direct, more with transfers in Pisa, 3-4.5 hours; an evening train—departing around 20:00—gives you a complete day in the region while still getting you to Rome that night), **Pisa** (about hourly, 1-1.5 hours), **Florence** (5/day direct, 2.5 hours, otherwise nearly hourly with change in Pisa), **Milan** (about hourly, 3 hours direct or with change in Genoa), **Venice** (about hourly, 5-6 hours, 1-3 changes).

From Monterosso by Train to: Venice (5/day, 6 hours, change in Milan), **Milan** (8/day direct, otherwise hourly with change in Genoa, 3-4 hours), **Genoa** (hourly, 1.2-2 hours), **Turin** (8/day, 3-4 hours), **Pisa** (hourly, 1-2 hours), **Sestri Levante** (hourly, 30 minutes, most trains to Genoa stop here), **La Spezia** (2-3/hour, 15-30 minutes), **Levanto** (2-3/hour, 4 minutes), **Santa Margherita Ligure** (at least hourly, 45 minutes), **Rome** (hourly, 4.5 hours, change in La Spezia). For destinations in **France,** change trains in Genoa.

BY CAR

Because these towns are close together and have frequent transportation connections, bringing a car to the Cinque Terre is not the best idea. If your plans require it, however, here are some basic tips: Stay in a hotel that includes parking, use public transportation or hike between towns, and for day-trip parking, go to Monterosso (€18/day), Riomaggiore (€23/day), or Manarola (€2/hour). Don't drive to Vernazza—the roads are in poor condition and the flood blew out its main parking lot. Parking anywhere on the Cinque Terre is truly a mess in July and August.

Milan to the Cinque Terre (130 miles): Drivers speed south on autostrada A-7 from Milan, skirt Genoa, and drive a little bit of Italy's curviest and narrowest freeways, passing the Cinque Terre toward the port of La Spezia (A-12). Another option is to take the slightly straighter A-1 via the city of Parma, followed by A-15 to La Spezia. This route takes the same amount of time (about 2.5 hours), even though it covers more miles.

The route from autostrada A-12 depends partly on the status of repairs to the 2011 flood damage. As of this writing (mid-2015), this is the best approach, but confirm details locally:

To reach **Monterosso** (about 30 minutes from the autostrada), exit A-12 at *uscita Carrodano-Levanto,* northwest of La Spezia. Remember that the road divides as you approach Monterosso—you must choose between the road to *Monterosso Centro Storico* (the old town) or the one to *Fegina* (the new town and beachfront parking). Keep in mind that because of road closures, you can't reach Monterosso from La Spezia via the other Cinque Terre towns; you'll have to loop up to the SP-1/SP-38 highway.

For **Vernazza, Riomaggiore, Corniglia,** or **Manarola,** leave the freeway at La Spezia and follow the road that parallels the coast (with access to each of these four towns). The drive down to Vernazza is scenic, narrow, and scary; it's much better to park in La Spezia and ride the train in. While there is a secondary road connecting Vernazza and Monterosso, it's likely closed and—even if open—it's not recommended.

Within the Cinque Terre: On busy weekends, holidays, and in June, July, and August, both Vernazza and Monterosso fill up, and police at the top of town will deny entry to anyone without a hotel reservation. It's smart to have a confirmation in hand.

Parking Tips: Riomaggiore, Manarola, and Monterosso each have parking lots and a shuttle bus to get you into town (described in those sections).

Blue signs post valid hours for pay parking (use cash), which usually don't charge from 24:00 to 8:00 (but read the signs or ask locals to be sure).

If you plan to find parking in any of the Cinque Terre towns, try to arrive between 9:00 and 11:00, when overnight visitors are usually departing. Or you can park your car in Levanto or La Spezia (both covered in next chapter), then take the train into the town of your choice. In these bigger towns, confirm that your parking spot is OK, and leave nothing inside to steal.

RIVIERA TOWNS NEAR THE CINQUE TERRE

Levanto • Sestri Levante • Santa Margherita Ligure •
Portofino • La Spezia • Carrara • Portovenere

The Cinque Terre is tops, but several towns to the north have a breezy beauty and more beaches. Towns to the south offer a mix of marble, trains, and yachts.

Levanto, the northern gateway to the Cinque Terre, has a long beach and a scenic, strenuous trail to Monterosso al Mare. Sestri Levante, on a narrow peninsula flanked by two beaches, is for sun-seekers. Santa Margherita Ligure is more of a real town, with actual sights, beaches, and easy connections with Portofino by trail, bus, or boat. All three towns are a straight shot to the Cinque Terre by train.

South of the Cinque Terre, you'll likely pass through the workaday town of La Spezia (don't stay here unless you're desperate), the southern gateway to the Cinque Terre. Carrara is a quickie for marble lovers who are driving between Pisa and La Spezia. The picturesque village of Portovenere, near La Spezia, has scenic boat connections with Cinque Terre towns.

Public transportation is the best way to get around this region. All the places in this chapter are well connected by train and/or boat.

North of the Cinque Terre

Levanto

Graced with a long, sandy beach, Levanto is packed in summer and popular with surfers. The rest of the year, it's just a small, sleepy town, with less charm and fewer tourists than the Cinque Terre. But with quick connections to Monterosso (4 minutes by train) and better dining options, Levanto makes a decent home base if you can't snare a room in the Cinque Terre.

Levanto has a new section (with a regular grid street plan) and a twisty old town (bisected by a modern street), plus a few pedestrian streets and a castle (not tourable). From Levanto, you can take a no-wimps-allowed hike to Monterosso (2.5 hours) or hop a boat to the Cinque Terre towns and beyond.

Orientation to Levanto

TOURIST INFORMATION

The helpful TI is on Piazza Cavour (daily 9:00-13:00 & 15:00-18:00 except Sun until 12:30, shorter hours off-season, tel. 0187-808-125, www.comune.levanto.sp.it). In peak season, the TI leads a weekly walking tour in English of Levanto's medieval architecture (free but tips expected, 2 hours, departs Thu at 18:00 from Piazza Cavour, register at TI).

ARRIVAL IN LEVANTO

By Train: It's a 10-minute walk from the Levanto train station to the TI in town (head down stairs in front of station, turn right, cross bridge, then follow Corso Roma to Piazza Mazzini).

By Car: Drivers can use cheap **short-term parking** in the lots in front of—and to either side of—the train station (€7.20/8 hours, €10.80/24 hours—pay at machines each day). Another option is the lot across the river from the hospital on the way into town (first left after the hospital, cross bridge and immediately turn left), or north of the church on Via del Mercato (free during high season, except

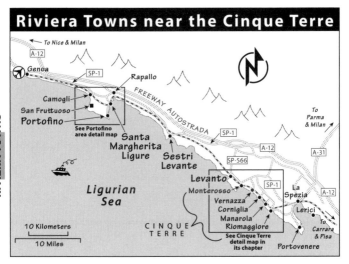

Wed before 14:00). For **long-term parking,** try the lots at Piazza Mazzini or behind the TI (€18/day).

HELPFUL HINTS

Markets: Levanto's modern covered *mercato,* which sells produce and fish, is on Via del Mercato, between the TI and train station (Mon-Sat 8:00-13:00, closed Sun). On Wednesday morning, an **open-air market** with clothes, shoes, and housewares fills the street in front of the *mercato.*

Internet Access: Try **Viaggi Beraldi** at Via Garibaldi 102 (€1.50/30 minutes, daily 9:00-13:00 & 16:00-20:00, tel. 0187-800-818).

Baggage Storage: None is available. Try La Spezia, Monterosso, Vernazza, or Santa Margherita Ligure.

Laundry: A **self-service launderette** stuffed with snack and drink vending machines is at Piazza Staglieno 38 (wash-€5 including soap, dry-€5, open 24 hours daily, mobile 338-701-6341). Another self-service place, **Speedy Wash,** is at Via Garibaldi 32 (wash-€5, dry-€2, daily 8:00-22:00, mobile 350-156-5026).

Bike Rental: Cicli Raso North Shore rents bikes (€10-20/day depending on type of bike, daily 9:30-12:30 & 15:30-19:30, closed Sun Nov-April, Via Garibaldi 63, tel. 0187-802-511, www.cicliraso.com). The **Sensafreni Bike Shop** is convenient to the beach boardwalk (€3/hour, €8/half-day, €15/24 hours, Mon-Sat 9:30-12:30 & 16:00-19:30, closed Sun, Piazza del Popolo 1, tel. 0187-807-128).

Sports Rentals: Rosa dei Venti rents kayaks, canoes, surfboards, and windsurfing equipment right on the beach (Marco's mobile 329-451-1981 or 335-608-9277, www.levantorosadeiventi.it).

Sights in Levanto

Beach

You can access Levanto's beach boardwalk and the sea right behind the TI. As you face the harbor, the boat dock is to your far left, and the diving center is to your far right (rental boats available at either place in summer). You can also rent a kayak or canoe on the beach, just below the east end of the Piazza Mazzini parking lot.

During the summer, three parts of the beach are free: both sides of the boat dock, and behind the TI. The rest of the beach is broken up into private sections that charge admission. You can always stroll along the beach, even through the private sections—just don't sit down. Off-season, roughly October through May, the entire beach is free, and you can lay your towel anywhere you like.

Old Town and Trailhead

The old town, several blocks from the TI and beach, clusters around Piazza del Popolo. Until a few decades ago, the town's open-air market was held at the 13th-century loggia (covered set of archways) in the square. Explore the back streets.

To reach the trailhead to Monterosso: From Piazza del Popolo, head uphill to the striped church, Chiesa di Sant'Andrea (with your back to the loggia, go straight ahead—across the square and up Via Don Emanuele Toso to the church). From the church courtyard, follow the sign to the *castello* (a private residence), go under the stone arch, and continue uphill. Or, if you're coming from the seaside promenade (Via Gaetano Semenza), head under the arches and up the stairs, and follow the signs to the *castello*. Either route leads you to a sign that points you toward Punta Mesco, the rugged tip of the peninsula. From here, you can hike up to Monterosso (2.5 hours). This lovely, rugged-and-wild hike is no joke—bring lots of water and wear good shoes. Most of the trail is a gradual up-and-down, but the last stretch into Monterosso is almost entirely big steps, so those with knee problems might consider starting in Monterosso instead. The elevation gain overall is more than double that of the toughest Cinque Terre hikes. The Cinque Terre hiking pass is not necessary here.

Hike or Bike to Bonassola and Beyond

Cross the river bridge located by the TI to wander along this easy waterfront path, good for walking or cycling. You'll encounter shaded tunnels and two sunny beaches on the way to the small but modern town of Bonassola with its sandy beach (25 minutes by foot, 10 minutes by bike, public beaches located a minute's walk down from trail). From Bonassola, the path continues on to the town of Framura, a 3.5-mile walk/ride from Levanto.

Sleeping in Levanto

In this popular beach town, many hotels want you to take half-pension (lunch or dinner) in summer, especially in July and August. Prices listed here are the maximum for high season (July-Aug); smaller rooms or those without views may be less. Expect to pay €10-30 less per night for April-June and September-October, and even less in November and March (most are closed Dec-Feb). The longer your stay, the greater your bargaining power. The high number of four-person rooms in Levanto makes it particularly welcoming to families. Many hotels rent out large apartments with kitchenettes (without a half-pension requirement), and parking is free or very reasonable.

$$$ Albergo Primavera is family-run, with 17 redecorated, tasteful rooms—10 with balconies but no views—just a half-block from the beach (Db-€130 if you book direct and pay cash, request a quiet room off the street, includes hearty breakfast buffet, air-con, parking-€10/day, free loaner bikes, Via Cairoli 5, tel. 0187-808-023, www.primaverahotel.com, info@primaverahotel.com; friendly Carlo, cheerful Daniela, and daughters Giuditta and Gloria).

$$$ Villa Margherita is 300 yards out of town, but the shady gardens, 11 characteristic colorfully tiled rooms, and tranquility are worth the walk (Db-€170, Tb-€185, 5 percent discount with cash, air-con, elevator one flight up from street level, free parking, 5-minute walk to train station, Via Trento e Trieste 31, tel. 0187-807-212, mobile 328-842-6934, www.villamargherita.net, info@villamargherita.net).

$$$ Garden Hotel offers 17 simple, bright, modern rooms, all with balconies (but most lack views), a block from the beach on busy Corso Italia (Db-€130, newer fifth-floor room with sea views and terrace-Db-€160, 5 percent discount with cash, closed Nov-mid-March, air-con, elevator for fifth floor only, free parking but not on-site, loaner bikes, Corso Italia 6, tel. 0187-808-173, www.nuovogarden.com, info@nuovogarden.com, Davide and Damiano).

$$$ Hotel Carla's 30 newer rooms, most with balconies, are decorated in soothing, neutral colors. It's located 5 minutes from the station and 10 minutes from the beach (Db-€140, air-con, Via Martiri della Libertà 28, tel. 0187-808-275, www.carlahotel.com, info@carlahotel.com).

$$ A Durmi is a happy little *affitta camere* (guesthouse) owned by lovely Graziella, Gianni, and their two daughters, Elisa and Chiara. Their sunny patios, green leafy gardens, six immaculate beach bungalow-type rooms, and five sunlit apartments make a

---

Sleep Code

Abbreviations   **(€1 = about $1.10, country code: 39)**
S=Single, **D**=Double/Twin, **T**=Triple, **Q**=Quad, **b**=bathroom
Price Rankings
  $$$ **Higher Priced**—Most rooms €110 or more
   $$ **Moderately Priced**—Most rooms between €50-110
    $ **Lower Priced**—Most rooms €50 or less
Unless otherwise noted, credit cards are accepted, breakfast
is included, free Wi-Fi and/or a guest computer is generally
available, and English is spoken. Many towns in Italy levy a
hotel tax of €1.50-5 per person, per night (often collected
in cash; usually not included in the rates I've quoted). Prices
change; verify current rates online or by email. For the best
prices, book directly with the hotel.

---

welcoming place to stay (Db-€110, Tb-€130; 3-4 person apartment-€160; ask about cash discount, breakfast-€8, air-con, bar, parking-€5/day, Via D. Viviani 12, tel. 0187-800-823, mobile 349-105-6016, www.adurmi.it, info@adurmi.it).

$$ Ristorante la Loggia has eight cozy yet somewhat musty rooms perched above the old loggia on Piazza del Popolo (Db-€70, cash only, request balcony, quieter rooms in back, two basic side-by-side apartments great for families of 4-8, lots of stairs, air-con, free parking, reception open 9:00-23:00, Piazza del Popolo 7, tel. 0187-808-107, mobile 335-641-7701, www.loggialevanto.com, Nerina does not speak English).

$$ Villa Clelia B&B offers five peaceful, dark, air-con rooms (named for the winds—*scirocco, maestrale,* and so on) with mini-fridges and terraces in a garden courtyard just 50 yards from the sea (Db-€100, minimal in-room breakfast, free parking; with loggia on your left, it's straight ahead at Piazza da Passano 1; tel. 0187-808-195, mobile 329-379-4859, www.villaclelia.it, info@villaclelia.it). They also have seven central apartments that economically sleep up to five (€700-850/week, 3-night minimum stay).

$$ La Rosa dei Venti is an *affitta camere* just a couple of blocks from the beach. Enthusiastic Rosanna and her son Marco rent five super-clean rooms with dark hardwood floors, comfy rugs, and a hodgepodge of glittery seashore decor (Db-€110, Tb-€135, includes homemade breakfast, air-con, free parking, across from Piazza del Popolo, Via della Compera, tel. 0187-808-165, Marco's mobile 328-742-8268, www.larosadeiventilevanto.com, info@larosadeiventilevanto.com).

$$ Agriturismo A Due Passi dal Mare is an in-town oasis, just a five-minute walk from the beach or the train station. Friendly Francesca and husband Maurizio rent four crisp, quiet rooms—with sizable bathrooms—in the 1920s home built by her grandfather; their back garden is open to guests (Sb-€50, Db-€80, Tb-€100, cheaper in spring and fall, free on-site parking, closed Jan-Feb, right on the main drag at Corso Roma 37, tel. 0187-809-177, mobile 338-960-1537, www.a2passidalmare.com, info@a2passidalmare.com).

$$ Hotel Dora has perfectly comfortable (if dated) rooms in a quiet residential neighborhood a 10-minute walk from the beach (Db-€100-125, Tb-€165, Qb-€185, Via Martiri della Libertà 27, tel. 0187-808-168, www.dorahotel.it, info@dorahotel.it).

Hostel: **$ Ostello Ospitalia del Mare,** a budget gem, is run by the city tourist association. It has 70 basic beds, airy rooms, an elevator, and a terrace in a well-renovated medieval palazzo a few steps from the old town (€25-30 beds in co-ed dorm rooms with private bath, Db-€68; includes breakfast, thin towels, and sheets; self-service laundry-€7.50, microwave, fridge, nonmembers welcome, no curfew, no lockout; office open daily April-Oct 8:00-13:00 & 16:00-20:00, until 23:00 weekend nights; may close Nov-March, Via San Nicolò 1, tel. 0187-802-562, www.ospitaliadelmare.it, info@ospitaliadelmare.it).

Eating in Levanto

Osteria Tumelin, a local favorite, is more expensive than other options, but has a dressy, sophisticated ambience and a wide selection of fresh seafood. Reservations are smart on weekends or to dine outside (€12-14 *primi,* €17-23 *secondi,* daily 12:00-15:00 & 19:00-22:30, closed Thu Oct-May, aquarium containing giant lobster and moray eels in first dining room on the right, Via D. Grillo 32, across street from loggia, tel. 0187-808-379, www.tumelin.it).

Da Rino, a small trattoria on a quiet pedestrian lane, dishes up reasonably priced fresh seafood and homemade Ligurian specialties prepared with care. Consider the grilled *totani* (squid), *pansotti con salsa di noci* (ravioli with walnut sauce), and *trofie al pesto* (local pasta with pesto sauce). Dine indoors or at one of the outdoor tables. On busy nights, they open up a second dining room across the street. Sommelier Anna will help you choose a good wine (€8-11 pastas, €13-16 *secondi,* Wed-Mon 19:00-22:00, closed Tue, Via Garibaldi 10, tel. 0187-813-475).

Ristorante la Loggia, next to the old loggia, makes fine food, including gnocchi with scampi and saffron sauce and a delectable seafood lasagna. Their daily fish specials are served in a homey, wood-paneled dining room or on a little terrace overlooking the square (€10-12 pastas, €10-16 *secondi,* daily 12:30-14:00 & 19:00-22:00, closed Nov-Feb, Piazza del Popolo 7, tel. 0187-808-107).

Ristorante Moresco serves large portions of pasta and sea-

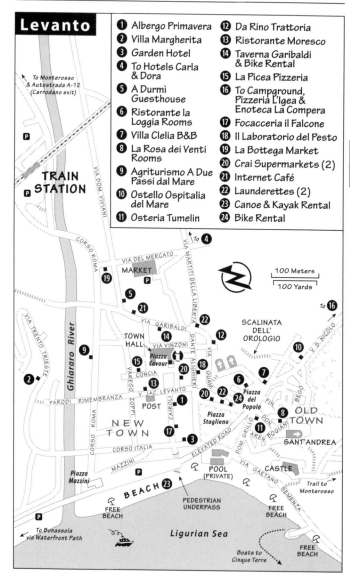

Levanto

1. Albergo Primavera
2. Villa Margherita
3. Garden Hotel
4. To Hotels Carla & Dora
5. A Durmì Guesthouse
6. Ristorante la Loggia Rooms
7. Villa Clelia B&B
8. La Rosa dei Venti Rooms
9. Agriturismo A Due Passi dal Mare
10. Ostello Ospitalia del Mare
11. Osteria Tumelin
12. Da Rino Trattoria
13. Ristorante Moresco
14. Taverna Garibaldi & Bike Rental
15. La Picea Pizzeria
16. To Campground, Pizzeria L'Igea & Enoteca La Compera
17. Focacceria il Falcone
18. Il Laboratorio del Pesto
19. La Bottega Market
20. Crai Supermarkets (2)
21. Internet Café
22. Launderettes (2)
23. Canoe & Kayak Rental
24. Bike Rental

food at reasonable prices in a vaulted, candlelit room decorated with Moorish-style frescoes. The best value is their €25 four-course tasting *menu* (doesn't include drinks, 2-person minimum, daily 12:00-14:00 & 19:00-21:00, reservations appreciated, Via Jacopo 24, tel. 0187-807-253, busy Roberto and Francesca).

Taverna Garibaldi is a good-value, cozy place on the most characteristic street in Levanto, serving focaccia with various toppings, made-to-order *farinata* (savory chickpea crêpe), over 30 types of pizza, and salads (€8-10 light meals, daily in summer 19:00-22:00, likely closed Tue Sept-June, Via Garibaldi 57, tel. 0187-808-098).

La Picea serves up wood-fired pizzas to go, or dine at one of their few small tables (Tue-Sun 12:00-14:00 & 18:00-24:00 or until they use up their pizza dough, closed Mon, just off the corner near Via Varego at Via della Concia 18, tel. 0187-802-063).

Pizzeria L'Igea is tucked just inside the Campeggio Acqua-dolce campground, 50 yards past the hostel. It's a favorite among locals who know you don't have to be a camper to enjoy freshly made, budget-conscious pizza. Their specialty is *gattafin*, deep-fried herb-stuffed ravioli (€3-9 pizzas, €7-9 pastas, daily 12:00-14:30 & 18:45-22:30, takeaway available, Via Guido Semenza 5, tel. 0187-807-293).

Enoteca La Compera offers a quiet respite on a hidden court-yard across the way from the campground. It's casual and friendly, serving a wide variety of panini (€3.50) that you can buy to-go, as well as plenty of wine. They also offer a *degustazione* (wine tast-ing) that costs €5 for 3 glasses or €10 for 6 glasses (March-Oct daily 10:00-20:00, follow the red-brick road—with little footprint stickers guiding the way—to Piazza della Compera 3, mobile 334-712-8517).

Picnics or Bites on the Go: *Focaccerie, rosticcerie,* and delis with takeout pasta abound on Via Dante Alighieri. **Focacceria il Falcone** has a great selection of focaccia with different toppings (daily 9:30-22:00, Oct-May closes at 20:00 and on Mon, Via Cai-roli 19, tel. 0187-807-370). For more picnic options, try the *mer-cato* (mornings except Sun). It's fun to grab a crusty loaf of bread, then pair it with a pot of freshly made Genovese pesto from **Il Laboratorio del Pesto** (sometimes closed Wed afternoons, Via Dante 14, tel. 0187-807-441). **La Bottega-Simply Market,** a short walk from the train station, has a good deli counter and is handy for those taking an early train (Mon-Sat 8:00-20:00, Sun 8:30-13:00). There are two **Crai supermarkets:** One is just off Via Jacopo da Levanto at Via del Municipio 5 (Mon-Sat 8:00-13:00 & 16:30-19:30, Sun 8:30-12:30); the other is nearby on Piazza Staglieno (for a shaded setting, lay out your spread on a bench in the grassy park at this piazza). Another excellent picnic spot is Piazza Cristoforo Colombo, located east of the swimming pool, with benches and sea views.

Levanto Connections

From Levanto: To get to the Cinque Terre, you can take the **train** (2-3/hour, 4 minutes to Monterosso). A slower, more scenic option is the **boat,** which stops at every Cinque Terre town—except Corniglia—before heading to Portovenere (April and June-Sept 2/day at 10:00 and 14:30; May Mon-Fri at 10:00, Sat-Sun at 14:30; none Nov-Easter; €7 one-way to Monterosso, 10:00 departure includes Cinque Terre, Portovenere, and Lerici Island tour for €28; 14:30 departure includes Cinque Terre and 1-hour stop in Portovenere for €22; 1 return boat each day from Portovenere departs at about 17:20; confirm locally—pick up boat schedule and price sheet from TI or boat dock, tel. 0187-732-987 or 0187-818-440, www.navigazionegolfodeipoeti.it).

Sestri Levante

This peninsular town is squeezed as skinny as a hot dog between its two beaches. The pedestrian-friendly Corso Colombo, which runs down the middle of the peninsula, is lined with shops that sell takeaway pizza, pastries, and beach paraphernalia. Don't be discouraged by the ugly modern town in front of the train station; the peninsula, about a seven-minute walk away, has charm to spare.

Hans Christian Andersen enjoyed his visit here in the mid-1800s, writing, "What a fabulous evening I spent in Sestri Levante!" One of the bays—Baia delle Favole—is named in his honor (*favole* means "fairy tale"). The small mermaid curled on the edge of the fountain behind the TI is another nod to the beloved Danish storyteller.

Orientation to Sestri Levante

Tourist Information: From the train station, it's a five-minute walk to the TI (Tue-Sat 9:30-12:45 & 13:30-17:00, closed Sun-Mon; go straight out of station on Via Roma, turn left at fountain in park, TI in next square at Piazza Sant'Antonio 10; tel. 0185-457-011). They can direct you to the trail (south of town) for a one-hour hike to the scenic Punta Manara promontory.

Market Day: It's on Saturday at Piazza Aldo Moro (8:00-13:00). Local producers of olive oil, cheese, jam, and honey also set up on occasional Sundays on Via Asilo Maria Teresa (where Via XXV Aprile and Corso Columbo meet).

Baggage Storage: None is available at the station.

Laundry: A self-service launderette is near the train station (wash-€5, daily 8:30-21:00, Via Costantino Raffo 8, mobile 329-012-8885).

Sights in Sestri Levante

Stroll the Town

From the TI, take Corso Colombo (to the left of Bermuda Bar, eventually turns into Via XXV Aprile, then Via alla Penisola), which runs up the peninsula. Follow this street—lively with shops, eateries, and delightful pastel facades—for about five minutes. Just before you get to Piazza Matteotti with the large white church at the end, turn off for either beach (free Silenzio beach is on your left). Or continue on the street to the left of the church and head uphill. You'll pass the evocative arches of a ruined chapel (bombed during World War II and left as a memorial). A few minutes farther on, past a stony Romanesque church, the road winds to the right to the Grand Hotel dei Castelli. The rocky, forested bluff at the end of the town's peninsula is actually the huge private backyard of this fancy hotel.

Beaches

These are named after the bays *(baie)* that they border. The bigger beach, **Baia delle Favole,** is divided up much of the year (May-Sept) into sections that you must pay to enter. Fees, which can soar up to €30 per day in August, generally include chairs, umbrellas, and fewer crowds. There are several small free sections: at the ends and in the middle (look for *libere* signs, and ask *"Gratis?"* to make sure that it's free). For less expensive sections of beach (where you can rent a chair for about €8-10), ask for *spiaggia libera attrezzata* (spee-AH-jah LEE-behr-ah ah-treh-ZAHT-tah). The usual beach-town activities are clustered along this *baia:* boat rentals, sailing lessons, and bocce courts—ask if you can get in on a game.

The town's other beach, **Baia del Silenzio,** is narrow, virtually all free, and packed, providing a good chance to see Italian families at play. There isn't much more to do here than unroll a beach towel and join in. At the far end of Baia del Silenzio (under Hotel Helvetia) is Citto Beach bar, which offers front-row seats with bay views (drinks daily June-Aug 10:00-24:00, May and Sept-Oct until 20:00, sandwiches and salads at lunchtime only, closed Nov-April, Gilberto).

Sleeping in Sestri Levante

Prices listed here are the maximum for the high season (July-Aug). Prices are €10-20 less per night April-June and September-October, and soft the rest of the year. Some hotels close off-season.

$$$ Hotel Helvetia, overlooking Baia del Silenzio, feels

Sestri Levante

To Rapallo & Santa Margherita Ligure

To Santa Margherita Ligure

TRAIN STATION

Piazza Caduti

To Santa Margherita Ligure & Portofino

To Cinque Terre

Ligurian Sea

To Cinque Terre

Piazza Italia

Baia delle Favole

Giardini Ventre

Piazza Sant' Antonio

To A-12 Freeway

Piazza Repubblica

BOAT DOCK

PROMENADE & BIKE PATH

Piazza Aldo Moro

VIA DELLA CHIUSA

GRAND HOTEL DEI CASTELLI

VICO CORO

Piazza Matteotti

FREE BEACH

Baia del Silenzio

ROMANESQUE CHURCH

RUINED CHAPEL

200 Meters
200 Yards

RIVIERA TOWNS

❶ Hotel Helvetia
❷ Hotel Celeste
❸ Hotel Mira
❹ Hotel Genova
❺ Albergo Marina
❻ Villa Jolanda
❼ L'Osteria Mattana

❽ Polpo Mario & Ristorante Mainolla
❾ Ice Cream's Angels
❿ Bacciolo Gelato
⓫ Tama Gelati e Molto di Più
⓬ Supermarkets (2)
⓭ Rosticceria Bertolone

posh and romantic, with 21 bright rooms, a large sun terrace with a heated, cliff-hanging swimming pool, and a peaceful garden atmosphere (viewless Db-€280, Db with sea view/balcony-€330, closed Nov-March, air-con, elevator, off-site parking-€20/day with free shuttle; from Corso Colombo, turn left on Via Palestro and angle left at the small square to Via Cappuccini 43, tel. 0185-41175, www.hotelhelvetia.it, helvetia@hotelhelvetia.it, Alex).

$$$ Hotel Celeste, a dream for beach lovers, rests along the waterfront. Its 41 rooms are modern and plainly outfitted—you pay for the sea breeze (Db-€185 with view and balcony, €25 optional half-pension, air-con, elevator, beach chairs deals, attached beachside bar, Lungomare Descalzo 14, tel. 0185-485-005, www. hotelceleste.com, info@hotelceleste.com, Franco).

$$$ Hotel Mira is an old-school hotel on the beachfront

promenade, just around the corner from the town's charming historical core and handy to the beaches. Rooms are simply furnished, yet have all amenities (Db-€150-160, Tb-€180-190, air-con, Viale Rimembranza 15, tel. 0185-459-404, www.hotelmira.com, info@hotelmira.com).

$$$ Hotel Genova, run by the Bertoni family, is a shipshape hotel with 19 shiny-clean, modern, and cheery rooms—three with sea view, sunny lounge, rooftop sundeck, free loaner bikes, and a good location just two blocks from Baia delle Favole (Sb-€75, Db-€130, superior Db-€150, Tb-€189, ask for quieter room in back, air-con, elevator, parking-€5/day; from the train station, walk straight ahead, turn right at the T-intersection, Viale Mazzini 126; tel. 0185-41057, www.hotelgenovasestrilevante.com, info@hotelgenovasestrilevante.com, Stefano).

$$ Albergo Marina's friendly Magda and her brother Santo rent 23 peaceful, and clean rooms done in sea-foam green. Though the hotel is located on a busy boulevard, rooms are at the back, facing a quiet courtyard and parking lots, and priced right (Db-€90, half-pension optional, air-con, elevator, free self-service laundry, pool table; exit the train station and angle left down Via Eraldo, at Piazza Repubblica, take an easy left onto Via Fasce and find the hotel ahead on the right, Via Fasce 100; tel. 0185-41527, www.marinahotel.it, marinahotel@marinahotel.it).

$$ Villa Jolanda is a homey, kid-friendly, bare-bones *pensione* with 17 dated rooms, five with little balconies but no views, and a garden courtyard/sun terrace—perfect for families on a budget... and the owner's cats (Sb-€45, Db-€90, Qb-€120, 3-night minimum stay required with advance reservation, owner Mario's €23 home-cooked dinners are worth it—available June-Aug with reservation, free parking; located near Baia del Silenzio—take alley just to the right of the church on Piazza Matteotti, Via Pozzetto 15, tel. 0185-41354, www.villajolanda.it, info@villajolanda.it).

Eating in Sestri Levante

Everything listed is on classic Via XXV Aprile, which also abounds with *focaccerie,* takeout pizza by the slice, and little grocery shops. Assemble a picnic or try one of the places below.

At **L'Osteria Mattana,** where everyone shares long tables in two dining rooms (the second one is in the back, past the wood oven and brazier), you can mix with locals while enjoying traditional cuisine, listed on chalkboard menus (Mon-Fri 19:30-22:30, Sat-Sun 12:30-14:30 & 19:30-22:30, no dinner served Mon Nov-April, cash only; follow Corso Colombo from TI as it turns into Via XXV Aprile, restaurant on right at #34; tel. 0185-457-633, Marco).

Polpo Mario is classier but affordable, with a fun people-watching location on the main drag (€8-15 pastas, €16-20 *secondi*, €40 fixed-price tasting *menu*, Tue-Sun 12:15-15:00 & 19:00-23:00, closed Mon, Via XXV Aprile 163, tel. 0185-480-203).

Ristorante Mainolla offers €6-8 pizzas, big salads, focaccia sandwiches, and reasonably priced pastas near Baia del Silenzio (daily 12:00-16:00 & 19:00-22:00, Via XXV Aprile 187, mobile 338-157-0877, tel. 0185-42792).

Gelato: There's no shortage of good gelato options. Tourists flock to **Ice Cream's Angels** at the intersection of Via XXV Aprile and Via della Chiusa. Riccardo and Elena artfully load up your cone and top it with a dollop of Nutella chocolate-hazelnut cream (open daily until late in summer, mobile 348-402-1604). **Bacciolo** enjoys a similar popularity among residents (closed Thu, Via XXV Aprile 51, on the right just before the church). **Tama Gelati e Molto di Più** makes their gelato onsite daily with fresh ingredients so you really taste the true flavors. *Mango* tastes like mango, *pera* tastes like pear, snozberries taste like snozberries...(near the beach at Baia delle Favole, Viale Rimembranza 34, mobile 347-777-4012).

Supermarket: You can stock up on picnic supplies at two **Carrefour Express** branches on Piazza della Repubblica, at #1 (Mon-Sat 8:00-13:00 & 15:30-19:30, closed Sun) and #28 (Mon-Sat 8:00-20:30, Sun 8:30-20:00).

Deli: For a takeout meal, head to **Rosticceria Bertolone** for roasted anything—beef, pork, chicken, or vegetables. Assemble an entire meal from their deli and ask them to heat it for you (Mon-Sat 7:30-13:00 & 16:00-19:30, closed Sun, Via Fascie Vincenzo 12, tel. 0185-487-098).

Sestri Levante Connections

By **train,** Sestri Levante is just 30 minutes away from Monterosso (hourly connections with Monterosso, nearly hourly with other Cinque Terre towns) and 30 minutes from Santa Margherita Ligure (2/hour).

Boats depart to the Cinque Terre, Santa Margherita Ligure, Portofino, and San Fruttuoso from the dock *(molo)* on the peninsula (boats run Easter-Oct; to get to the dock: facing the church in Piazza Matteotti, take the road on the right with the sea on your right, about halfway down Via Pilade Queirolo; tel. 0185-284-670, mobile 336-253-336, www.traghettiportofino.it).

Santa Margherita Ligure

If you need the Riviera of movie stars, park your yacht at Portofino. Or you can settle down with more elbow room in nearby and more personable Santa Margherita Ligure (15 minutes by bus from

Portofino and one hour by train from the Cinque Terre). While Portofino's velour allure is tarnished by a nonstop traffic jam in peak season, Santa Margherita tumbles easily downhill from its train station. The town has a fun Old World resort character and a breezy harborfront with a beach promenade.

On a quick day trip from Milan or the Cinque Terre, walk the beach promenade and see the small old town of Santa Margherita Ligure before catching the bus (or boat) to Portofino to see what all the fuss is about. With more time, Santa Margherita makes a fine overnight stop or home base for hiking the Portofino peninsula.

Orientation to Santa Margherita Ligure

TOURIST INFORMATION

The TI is as central as can be (at the harborside of the city traffic hub, Piazza Veneto). They know the questions and have the answers. The ATP bus office is next door, and bus #82 to Portofino stops at the curb in front (April-Sept daily 9:30-12:30 & 14:30-19:30, Oct-March closes at 17:30 and all day Sun, tel. 0185-287-485, www.turismoinliguria.it).

ARRIVAL BY TRAIN

The station itself is a pleasant, low-stress scene. To avoid waiting in line, buy your departure ticket before leaving the station. The bar/café (facing track 1) functions as a TI and welcome center (selling bus, train, and sightseeing-boat tickets with no commission and storing bags). Enjoy its crazy clocks while you sip an espresso awaiting your train.

To get from the station to the city center, take the stairs marked *Mare* (sea) down to the harbor; or head more gently down Via Roma which leads to the town center, TI, start of my town walk, and recommended hotels (about 10 minutes away on foot).

Bus #82 to Portofino stops a few steps below the station (2/hour, €1.80 from station bar/café, €2.80 from driver).

HELPFUL HINTS

Post Office: It's down the road from the train station at Via Roma 36 (Mon-Fri 8:20-19:05, Sat 8:20-12:35, closed Sun).

Baggage Storage: There's no official left-luggage office here, but the bar/café at the train station will store bags (€2.50/day).

Pharmacy: One is on pedestrian-only Via Palestro (closed Thu), and another at the corner of Piazza Caprera and Via Pescino, not far from the TI.

Laundry: Close to Piazza Mazzini is **Bolle Blu** (daily 7:00-22:30, €5/wash, €2/dry-10 minutes, includes soap, Via Roccatagliata 39, mobile 335-642-7203).

Bike Rental: GM Rent is at Via XXV Aprile 11 (€10/5 hours, €20/24 hours, also rents scooters and Smart Cars, daily 10:00-13:00 & 16:30-20:00, mobile 329-406-6274, www.gmrent.it, Francesco).

Taxi: Taxis wait outside the train station and charge €15 for a ride to anywhere in town, €25 to Paraggi beach, and €35 to Portofino (tel. 0185-286-508). Most recommended hotels are an easy 10-minute walk downhill from the station.

Driver: Helpful taxi driver **Alessandro** has five cars and two minivans and offers airport transfers to Genoa, Milan, Florence, and Nice. He is also available for local excursions, including all-day trips to the Cinque Terre (mobile 338-860-2349, www. alessandrotaxi.com, alessandrotaxi@yahoo.it).

Parking: Ask your hotel about parking (some have free spots). Otherwise, try a private lot (about €15/half-day, €20/24 hours) such as **Autopark,** next to the post office (Via Roma 38, tel. 0185-287-818). An hourly parking lot is by the harbor, in front of the fish market (pay-and-display, €2.50/hour). Parking is generally free where there are white lines; blue lines mean you pay.

Local Guide: Roberta De Beni is good (€100/half-day, €165/day, mobile 349-530-4778, diodebe@inwind.it).

Santa Margherita Ligure Walk

Get your bearings and cover the basics of Santa Margherita Ligure with this little self-guided walk.

• *Start at the square facing the exuberant Baroque facade of the Basilica of Santa Margherita.*

Piazza Caprera: Each day this square hosts a few farmers selling their produce. On the corner of Via Cavour, just next to

RIVIERA TOWNS

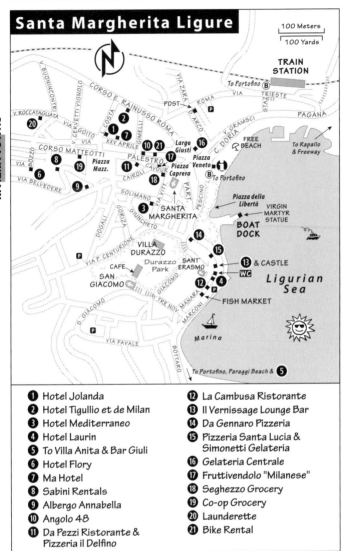

Santa Margherita Ligure

100 Meters
100 Yards

TRAIN STATION

To Portofino

V. BUONINCONTRI
CORSO E. RAINUSSO
V. ROCCATAGLIATA
VIA CERVETTI VIGNOLO
VIA COSTA
VIA GOITO
CORSO MATTEOTTI
XXV APRILE
GIMELLI
PALESTRO
CAIROLI
VIA CAVOUR
LA VITT.
PARTIG.
SOLIMANO
GIUNCHETO
GORZA
DUGALI
VIA P. CENTURIONE
VIA GIACOMO
TRE NOV.
MAVARA
S. GIACOMO
VIA FAVALE
BOTTARO
MARCONI
VIA ZARA
VIA ARCO
ROMA
VIA STAZ.
TRIESTE
PAGANA
C. DORIA
C. GRAMSCI
FESCINO
VIA BELVEDERE
VIA BOZZO

POST

Largo Giusti
Piazza Mazz.
Piazza Caprera
Piazza Veneto

SANTA MARGHERITA

FREE BEACH

To Rapallo & Freeway

To Portofino

Piazza della Libertà

VIRGIN MARTYR STATUE

BOAT DOCK

VILLA DURAZZO
Durazzo Park
CAFE
SAN GIACOMO
SANT' ERASMO

& CASTLE
WC
FISH MARKET

Ligurian Sea

Marina

To Portofino, Paraggi Beach & ⑤

1. Hotel Jolanda
2. Hotel Tigullio et de Milan
3. Hotel Mediterraneo
4. Hotel Laurin
5. To Villa Anita & Bar Giuli
6. Hotel Flory
7. Ma Hotel
8. Sabini Rentals
9. Albergo Annabella
10. Angolo 48
11. Da Pezzi Ristorante & Pizzeria il Delfino
12. La Cambusa Ristorante
13. Il Vernissage Lounge Bar
14. Da Gennaro Pizzeria
15. Pizzeria Santa Lucia & Simonetti Gelateria
16. Gelateria Centrale
17. Fruttivendolo "Milanese"
18. Seghezzo Grocery
19. Co-op Grocery
20. Launderette
21. Bike Rental

the basilica, visit **Seghezzo,** a venerable grocer where locals know they'll find whatever they need (described later, under "Eating in Santa Margherita Ligure").

• *Now take a side trip right up the "via principale" or main drag of the city, Via Palestro/Via Cavour. You'll go two blocks up to Piazza Mazzini and back.*

"*Via Principale*": The main "street" here is really two parallel streets divided by very tall and skinny buildings. We'll start by taking Via Cavour on the left and come back on Via Palestro. As you walk, study the characteristic, Art Nouveau house-painting from the turn of the last century. Before 1900, people distinguished their buildings with pastel paint and distinctive door and window frames. Then they decided to get fancy and paint entire exteriors with false balconies, weapons, saints, beautiful women, and 3-D Gothic effects.

Strolling up Via Cavour, look through the skinny shops on the right, which also front Via Palestro. You'll pass a traditional *panificio* (bakery; there's another at Via Palestro #34) where you can say, *"Vorrei un etto di focaccia"* to treat yourself to about a quarter-pound of the region's famed, olive-oily bread (€1, plenty for two).

Where the two streets merge is the recommended and popular **Angolo 48** restaurant (you might reserve a table for dinner as you pass by). Continue strolling to the big square, Piazza Mazzini, then return on Via Palestro to Piazza Caprera and the big church. For good produce and glass-jarred delicacies, I like **Fruttivendolo "Milanese"** (at Via Palestro 13). The family and community feel all along here is a joy.

• *See you back at the church.*

Basilica of Santa Margherita: The town's main church is textbook Italian Baroque (free, daily 7:30-12:00 & 15:00-18:30). Its 18th-century facade hides a 17th-century interior slathered with art and dripping with chandeliers. The altar is typical of 17th-century Ligurian altars—shaped like a boat, with lots of shelf space for candles, flowers, and relics. Its centerpiece is a much venerated statue of Our Lady of the Rose. She's adorned this altar since 1756 and is credited with lots of miracles.

Baroque is theater...and this altar is stagecraft. After the Vatican II decrees of the 1960s, priests began to face their flocks instead of the old altars. For this reason, all over the Catholic world, modern tables serving as post-Vatican II altars stand in front of earlier altars, like the one here, that are no longer the center of attention during the Mass.

Wander the church and its chapels, noticing the inlaid-marble floors and sparkling glass chandeliers. As you marvel at the richness, remember that the region's aristocrats amassed wealth from trade in the 11th to the 15th centuries. When Constantinople fell to the Turks, free trade in the Mediterranean stopped, and Genovese traders became bankers—making even more money. A popular saying of the day was, "Silver is born in America, lives in Spain, and dies in Genoa." Bankers here served Spain's 17th-century royalty and aristocracy, and the accrued wealth paid for a Golden Age of art.

• *Walk straight in front of the church a block to busy Largo Antonio Giusti. Next to the cinema (across the street), a penguin marks a recommended*

RIVIERA TOWNS

gelateria. *Head right to Piazza Veneto, with its busy roundabout and little park on the harbor. In the park facing the roundabout stands the TI, ATP bus office, and a bus #82 stop for Portofino.*

Beachfront Promenade: Stroll to the left along Corso Doria. The sidewalk is wider than the street, an indication that for more than 100 years this has been the place to promenade under century-old pastel facades. You'll pass the grand old **Lido Palace Hotel** with its view balconies overlooking a crowded beach scene.

• *Turn around and go back to Piazza Veneto. Continue walking the other direction along the water toward the little castle.*

You'll pass a rack of metal panels limiting political advertising for each party (great idea wouldn't you say?). Next comes a Christopher Columbus statue. He was born "Cristoforo Colombo" in 1451 in Genoa, near here—although some claim he was Spanish or Portuguese—and first sailed on Genovese boats along this Ligurian coast. Next comes a statue of King Victor Emmanuel II, always ready to brandish his sword and create Italy.

• *Before arriving at the castle, head out the little pier with the white statue facing out to sea.*

View from the Pier: From here, standing with "Santa Margherita Virgin Martyr," you can take in all of Santa Margherita Ligure—from the villas dotting the hills, to the castle built in the 16th century to defend against Saracen pirates, to the exclusive hotels. Tourist boats depart from this pier.

• *Continue along the waterfront on Corso Marconi.*

Harbor and Fish Market: Notice the trendy, recommended Il Vernissage Lounge Bar with tables up at the base of the castle. Continuing around the corner from the castle (closed to visitors), walk along the harbor. The region's largest fishing fleet—20 boats—ties up here. The fishing industry survives, drag-netting octopus, shrimp, and miscellaneous "blue fish." (Anchovies are no longer fished from here but from nearby Sestri Levante). The fish market (Mercato del Pesca, across the street, inside the rust-colored building with arches and columns) wiggles weekdays from about 16:00 until 20:00 or so—depending on who's catching what and when. It's a cool scene as fishermen take bins of freshly caught fish directly to waiting customers.

• *Climb the narrow brick stairs just to the right of the fish market to a delightful little square. Find the characteristic, black-and-white pebble mosaic and relax on the benches to enjoy harbor views. Facing the square is the little...*

Oratory of Sant'Erasmo: Named for St. Erasmus, the protector of sailors, this church is actually an "oratory," where a brotherhood of faithful men who did anonymous good deeds congregated and worshipped. While rarely open, do check. The interior is decorated with ships and paintings of storms that—

Rise of a Resort: The History of Santa Margherita Ligure

This town, like the entire region (from the border of France to La Spezia), was once ruled by the Republic of Genoa. In the

16th century, when Arab pirates from North Africa plagued the entire coastal area, Genoa built castles in the towns and lookout towers in the neighboring hills.

At the time, Santa Margherita was actually two bickering towns—each with its own bay. In 1800, Napoleon came along, took over the Republic of Genoa, and turned the rival towns into one city—naming it Porto Napoleone. When Napoleon fell in 1815, the town stayed united and took the name of the patron saint of its leading church, Santa Margherita.

In 1850, residents set to work creating a Riviera resort. They imported palm trees from North Africa and paved a fine beach promenade. Santa Margherita (and the surrounding area) was studded with fancy villas built by the aristocracy of Genoa (which was controlled by just 35 families). English, Russian, and German aristocrats also discovered the town in the 19th century. Mass tourism only hit in the last generation. Even with the increased crowds, the town decided to stay chic and kept huge developments out. Its neighbor, Rapallo, chose the extreme opposite—giving the Italian language a new word for uncontrolled growth ruining a once-cute town: *rapallizzazione*.

thanks to St. Erasmus—the local seafarers survived. The huge crosses standing in the nave are carried through town on special religious holidays.

• *Your walk is over. For a little extra exercise and to see a delightful park, climb the long stairs from here up to the Church of San Giacomo (with an interior similar to the Basilica of Santa Margherita) and Durazzo Park (described later).*

Sights in Santa Margherita Ligure

Durazzo Park (Parco di Villa Durazzo)

This park was an abandoned shambles until 1973, when the city took it over. Today it's a delight, with a breezy café, a carefully coiffed Italian garden (designed to complement the villa's architecture), and the intentionally wild "English garden" below (park entry free, daily 9:00-19:00 or 20:00, closes earlier off-season, WC near café). The Italian garden is famous for its varied collection of palm trees and an extensive collection of camellias. It's OK to feed the large turtles in the central pond (they like bits of fish or meat). The park is dominated by Villa Durazzo, the home of the late journalist/writer Vittorio Rossi; it's not worth touring but hosts concerts—mostly in summer.

Beaches

The handiest free Santa Margherita beaches are just below the train station toward the boat dock. But the best beaches are on the south side of town. Among these, I like "Gio and Rino beach" (just before Covo di Nord Est)—not too expensive, with fun, creative management and a young crowd. Also nice is the beach on the south side of Hotel Miramare, which offers a more relaxing sun-worshipping experience. Both beaches have free entry and rentable chairs and umbrellas. They're a 20-minute walk from downtown, or take the bus from either the train station or Piazza Veneto (bus tickets-€1.80, €2.80 from driver).

Paraggi beach, which is halfway to Portofino (with an easy bus connection—see "Portofino," later in this chapter), is better than any Santa Margherita beach, but it's *very* expensive. One Paraggi beach operator, Bosetti, offers a reasonable rate (€25/day, no hourly rates, includes umbrella, lounge chair, and towel), while rates at other places may soar up to €50 per day in July and August. In high season, the Paraggi beach may be all booked up by big shots from Portofino, which has no beach—only rocks. Off-season, the entire Paraggi beach is all yours and free of charge. A skinny patch of sand smack-dab in the middle of Paraggi beach is free year-round. Locals prefer hopping the train for Camogli (west) and Sestri Levanto (east).

Portofino Side-Trip

One of the most beautiful and famous little Mediterranean resorts—Portofino—is just a couple miles down the coast and is so easy to visit from Santa Margherita that it can be considered a town sight.

Sleeping in Santa Margherita Ligure

All of these accommodations are in the center of town. Hotel Jolanda and Hotel Tigullio et de Milan are closest to the station. Prices listed here are the maximum price for the high season of July-August. Prices drop a lot off-season.

$$$ Hotel Jolanda is a solid, professionally run hotel with 50 rooms, a revolving door, and a friendly staff. With lavish public spaces and regal colors, this place makes you feel like nobility (Db-€150, superior Db-€175, 10 percent direct-booking discount with this book, air-con, elevator, free use of small weight room, wet and dry saunas, free loaner bikes, Via Luisito Costa 6, tel. 0185-287-512, www.hoteljolanda.it, info@hoteljolanda.it).

$$$ Hotel Tigullio et de Milan has equally fine rooms with creamy hues and lower prices. You don't get all the luxurious extras, but the breezy sun terrace on top—with a bar in summertime—makes for a relaxing retreat (Db-€140, bigger Db with terrace-€160, 10 percent direct-booking discount with this book, air-con, elevator, a few free parking spots, free loaner bikes, Via Rainusso 3, tel. 0185-287-455, www.hoteltigullio.eu, info@hoteltigullio.eu).

$$$ Hotel Mediterraneo, run by the Melegatti family, offers 30 spacious rooms (a few with balconies or sun terraces) in a family-friendly, creaky, and comfy 18th-century palazzo a five-minute walk from Piazza Veneto. They have a park-like sun garden with lounge chairs and lots of semiprivate space. Kindly Pia Pauli presides over the dining room and makes great homemade Ligurian specialties for dinner (Sb-€105, Db-€155, Tb-€185, extensive breakfast, five-course dinner-€35/person, half the rooms have air-con, free parking, closed Dec-March, behind Basilica of Santa Margherita at Via della Vittoria 18A, tel. 0185-286-881, www.sml-mediterraneo.it, info@sml-mediterraneo.it).

$$$ Hotel Laurin offers slick, modern, air-conditioned, pricey American-style lodgings fixated on harborfront views. All of its 43 rooms face the sea, most have terraces, and a small pool is on the sundeck, as well as a gym. Enrico and staff are helpful (Sb-€183, Db-€252, Tb-€350, Qb-€406, request a 10 percent direct-booking discount with this book, double-paned windows, elevator, air-con, parking-€18/day, just past the castle, Corso Marconi 3, tel. 0185-289-971, www.laurinhotel.it, info@laurinhotel.it).

$$$ Villa Anita is an elegant-yet-homey family hotel run by Daniela and her son, Sandro. They rent 12 tidy rooms—nearly all with terraces and most with new, high-tech bathrooms—overlooking a peaceful residential neighborhood a five-minute uphill walk from the seaside boulevard. The in-house chef offers a varying menu of Ligurian specialties (Db-€170, superior Db-€200, dinner-€25/person except Mon, family rooms, playground, small gym, small heated pool and sauna, air-con, free parking, closed in winter, Viale Minerva 25, tel. 0185-286-543, www.hotelvillaanita.com, info@hotelvillaanita.com).

$$$ Spanning two buildings, **Hotel Flory** is a basic 16-room hotel with thin walls, surrounded by flowers and greenery. It's run enthusiastically by Florinda (who wants to practice her English with you) and Enrico, whose three kids make this a family-friendly place (Sb-€80, Db-€120, Tb-€150, Qb-€180, four rooms have balconies, small public patio, no elevator, rooftop terrace, free loaner bikes, laundry service-€15, parking-€20/day, 10-minute walk from station at Via Bozzo 3, tel. 0185-286-435, www.hotelflory.it, hotelflory@hotelflory.it).

$$$ Ma Hotel is a charming boutique spot along a busy road, with 11 clean, spacious, and swanky rooms (Db-€160-175, extra bed-€30, breakfast-€10, air-con, patio, loaner bikes, Via XXV Aprile 18, www.mahotel.it, info@mahotel.it).

$$ Sabini Rentals, charmingly run by Cristina, offers three renovated rooms and one apartment with a tiny corner kitchen (Db-€88, Tb-€105, Qb-€125, breakfast extra, 2-night minimum, cash only, book direct and ask for a Rick Steves discount, Via Belvedere 31, mobile 338-902-7582, www.sabinirentals.com, info@sabinirentals.com).

$$ Albergo Annabella has nine rooms (some with shared bath) that are funky and stark but are a good budget option. Owner Annabella speaks some English (S-€35, Sb-€50, D-€70, Db-€100, some with air-con, Via Costasecca 10, mobile 380-328-0542, tesibruno@gmail.com).

Eating in Santa Margherita Ligure

IN THE CITY CENTER

Angolo 48, run by savvy Elisa and Valentina, serves hearty yet beautifully presented—and reasonably priced—Genovese and Ligurian dishes from a creative and accessible menu. At this cool-without-the-pretense locale, you feel part of something new and appetizing. Reservations are important; there's great seating both on the square and inside. Try their handmade *pansotti* in walnut sauce (€8-11 salads and *antipasti*, €9-14 pastas, €16-20 *secondi* and nightly specials, always gluten-free pasta and vegan options, lunch served Tue-Wed and Sat-Sun, dinner nightly 18:15-22:00, Via Palestro 48, tel. 0185-286-650).

Da Pezzi, with a cheap cafeteria-style atmosphere, is packed with locals at midday and at night. They're munching *farinata* (crêpes made from chickpeas, available Oct-May 18:00-20:00) standing at the bar, or enjoying pesto and fresh fish in the dining room. Consider the deli counter with its Genovese picnic ingredients (Sun-Fri 10:00-14:00 & 17:00-21:00, closed Sat, Via Cavour 21, tel. 0185-285-303, Giancarlo and Giobatta).

ON THE WATERFRONT

La Cambusa, perched above the fish market, is popular for its sea-food. While the food is forgettable, the view from its harborside terrace is not. In cooler weather, the terrace is covered and heated. Diners receive a free glass of *Sciacchetrà* (local dessert wine) and biscotti with this book (€12-16 pastas, €18-25 *secondi*, July-Sept daily 12:00-15:00 & 19:00-24:00, closed Thu off-season, Via Tommaso Bottaro 1, tel. 0185-287-410, www.ristorantelacambusa.net).

All along the harbor side of Via Tommaso Bottaro, south of the marina, you'll find restaurants, pizzerias, and bars serving food with a nautical view. **Bar Giuli,** the only place actually on the water, serves forgettable salads and sandwiches for a reasonable price (about 150 yards south of the fish market, where Via Maragliano meets Via Garibaldi).

At **Il Vernissage Lounge Bar,** you can nurse your €8 drink with a million-dollar view. There are 20 wines by the glass, plus cocktails and spritzes, which always come with a nice plate of finger food (March-Oct daily until late, Salita al Castello 8, mobile 349-220-5846, Sandro).

BUDGET OPTIONS

Pizzeria il Delfino serves thin, big, wood-fired pizzas nightly from 19:00. It's a rustic and fun local scene with tight inside seating and a few quiet tables outside (€8 pizzas, Via Cavour 29, tel. 0185-286-488).

Two fancier pizzerias, side by side on Piazza della Libertà near the harbor, are also popular. **Da Gennaro Pizzeria** is big and bright (at #30, tel. 0185-286-951); **Pizzeria Santa Lucia** is more relaxed and intimate (at #42, tel. 0185-287-163).

Gelato: The best *gelateria* I found in town—with chocolate-truffle *tartufato*—is **Simonetti** (daily 8:30 until late, under the castle, closest to the water at Piazza della Libertà 48, Margherita will win you over with samples). **Gelateria Centrale,** just off Piazza Veneto near the cinema, serves up their specialty—*pinguino* (penguin), a cone with your choice of gelato dipped in chocolate (daily 8:30-late).

Groceries: **Seghezzo** is classiest and great for a meal to go—ask them to *riscaldare* (heat up) their white *lasagne al pesto* or dish up their special *carpaccio di polpo*—thinly sliced octopus (daily June-Aug 7:30-13:00 & 15:30-20:00, closed Wed Sept-May, right of the church on Via Cavour, tel. 0185-287-172). The **Co-op** grocery, off Piazza Mazzini at Corso Giacomo Matteotti 9, is cheaper and less romantic (daily 8:15-13:00 & 15:30-19:30). Either is a good place to stock up on well-priced Ligurian olive oil, pasta, and pesto.

Santa Margherita Ligure Connections

From Santa Margherita Ligure by Train to: Sestri Levante (2/ hour, 30 minutes), **Monterosso** (hourly, 45 minutes), **La Spezia** (hourly, 1-1.5 hours), **Pisa** (1-2/hour, 2 hours, most connections with transfer, less frequent InterCity/IC goes direct), **Milan** (about hourly, 2.5 hours, more with transfer in Genoa), **Ventimiglia/ French border** (4/day, 4 hours; or hourly with change in Genoa), **Venice** (at least hourly, 6 hours with changes). For **Florence,** transfer in Pisa (8/day, 4 hours).

By Boat to the Cinque Terre: Tour boats make various trips to Vernazza, Portovenere, and other ports about daily for around €20. For the latest, pick up a schedule of departures and excursion options from the TI, visit the ticket shack on the dock, call mobile 336-253-336, or check online at www.traghettiportofino.it.

Portofino

Santa Margherita Ligure, with its aristocratic architecture, hints at old money, whereas nearby Portofino, with its sleek shops, has the sheen of new money. Fortunately, a few pizzerias, *focaccerie,*

bars, and grocery shops are mixed in with Portofino's jewelry shops, art galleries, and haute couture boutiques, making the town affordable. The *piccolo* harbor, classic Italian architecture, and wooded peninsula can turn glitzy

Portofino into an appealing package. It makes a fun day trip from Santa Margherita Ligure.

Ever since the Romans founded Portofino for its safe harbor, it has had a strategic value (appreciated by everyone from Napoleon to the Nazis). In the 1950s, *National Geographic* did a beautiful exposé on the idyllic port, and locals claim that's when the Hollywood elite took note. Liz Taylor and Richard Burton came here annually (as did Liz Taylor and Eddie Fisher). During one famous party, Rex Harrison dropped his Oscar into the bay (it was recovered). Ava Gardner came down from her villa each evening for a drink—sporting her famous fur coat. Greta Garbo loved to swim naked in the harbor, not knowing that half the town was watching. Truman Capote also called Portofino home. But VIPs were also here a century earlier. In one of his books,

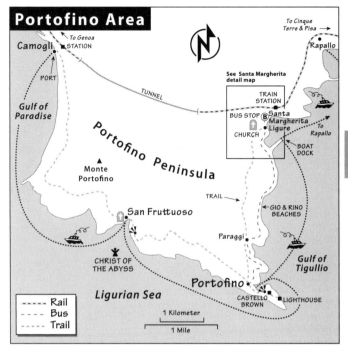

Friedrich Nietzsche wrote about philosophizing with the mythical prophet Zarathustra on the path between Portofino and Santa Margherita.

My favorite Portofino plan: Visit for the evening. Leave Santa Margherita on the bus at about 16:30 and hike the last 20 minutes from Paraggi beach. Explore Portofino. Splurge for a drink on the harborfront, or get a takeout fruity sundae (*paciugo;* pah-CHOO-goh) and sit by the water. Then return by bus to Santa Margherita for dinner (confirm late departures). Portofino offers all kinds of harborside dining, but the quality often doesn't match the high prices. If you do decide to eat in Portofino, **Ristorante lo Stella,** just a few steps from the boat dock, has well-prepared dishes, friendly servers, and portholes in the bathrooms. Opposite the boat dock, little **Calata 32** dishes up cones and cups.

GETTING TO PORTOFINO

Portofino makes an easy day trip from Santa Margherita by bus, boat, bike, or foot.

By Bus: Catch bus #82 from Santa Margherita's train station or at bus stops along the harbor (main stop in front of TI, €1.80, 2/hour, 15 minutes, goes to Paraggi or Portofino). Buy tickets at the train station bar, at Piazza Veneto's green bus kiosk (next to

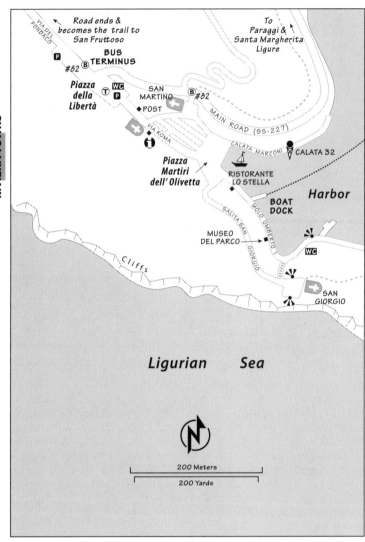

the TI; daily 7:00-19:30), from the green machine on the side of
the kiosk, or at any newsstand, tobacco shop, or shop that displays
a *Biglietti Bus* sign (or on the bus for €2.80). If you're at the Piazza Veneto kiosk, grab a bus schedule to plan your return (last bus
around 23:00).

In Portofino, get tickets at the newsstand or tobacco store on
Piazza della Libertà, or from the machine next to the bus stop (go
uphill from the harbor and you'll come to the piazza—newsstand
and tobacco store on the left side; ticket machine and bus stop on
the right).

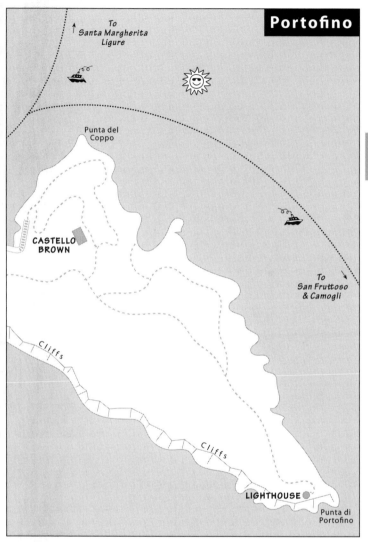

By Taxi: Taxi stands in Santa Margherita are at the train station and down by the water on Via Pescino, not far from TI (around €35 to Portofino).

By Boat: The boat makes the 15-minute trip with more class and without the traffic jams (€6 one-way, €9 round-trip; hourly departures April-Oct daily 10:15-16:15, fewer departures off-season; dock is a 2-minute walk from Piazza Veneto off Piazza Martiri della Libertà, call to confirm or pick up schedule from TI or your hotel, tel. 0185-284-670, mobile 336-253-336, check at www.traghettiportofino.it).

By Bike: The 25-minute bike ride from Santa Margherita to Portofino is doable for cautious cyclists. While there are no steep hills to struggle up, the road is narrow, with many blind corners. Many of my recommended hotels provide free loaner bikes (though they may not be in the best condition); you can also rent your own wheels.

On Foot: To hike the entire distance from Santa Margherita Ligure to Portofino, you have two options: You can follow the sidewalk along (and sometimes hanging over) the sea (1 hour, 2.5 miles)—although traffic can be noisy, and in places, the footpath disappears. Or, if you're hardy and ambitious, you can take a quieter two-hour hike by leaving Santa Margherita at Via Maragliano, then follow the Ligurian-symbol trail markers (look for red-and-white stripes—they're not always obvious, sometimes numbered according to the path you're on, usually painted on rocks or walls, especially at junctions). This hike takes you high into the hills. Keep left after Cappelletta delle Gave. Several blocks past a castle, you'll drop down into the Paraggi beach, where you'll take the Portofino trail the rest of the way.

Bus and Hike Option: For a shorter hike (20 minutes) into Portofino, ride bus #82 from Santa Margherita only as far as the small but ritzy Paraggi beach. (Ask on board where to get off—watch for an inland bay with green water and a sandy beach.) At the far end of the beach, cross the street, climb the steps, and follow the hilly, paved trail marked *Pedonale per Portofino* high above the road. Twenty minutes later, you'll enter Portofino at a yellow-and-gray-striped church labeled *Divo Martino*—which I figure means "the divine Martin" and has something to do with Dean Martin giving us all "Volare" (which I couldn't get out of my head for the rest of the day).

Orientation to Portofino

Tourist Information: Portofino's TI is under a portico, uphill from the boat dock and downhill from the bus stop. Pick up a free town map and a rudimentary hiking map (June-Sept Tue-Sun 10:00-13:00 & 14:00-18:00, closed Mon; Oct-May Tue-Sat 9:30-13:30 & 13:15-17:00, closed Sun-Mon; Via Roma 35, tel. 0185-269-024).

Sights in Portofino

Museo del Parco

For an artsy break, walk around the harbor to the right, where you can stroll around a park littered with 148 contemporary sculptures by mostly Italian artists, including a few top names (€5, June-Oct Wed-Mon 10:00-13:30 & 15:00-20:00, closed Tue, closed Nov-May and in bad weather, mobile 337-333-737, www.museodiportofino.it).

Hikes

One option is the paved stone path that winds up and down to the **lighthouse** *(faro)* at a scenic point with a bar (take the stairs on the right just after Museo del Parco, bar open May-Sept, hedges block views until the end, 25-minute walk). Consider popping into **Castello Brown,** a medieval castle, on the way up or down. It features lush gardens, sweeping viewpoints, and special exhibits about Portofino and its history. Minimal original decorations and exhibits are explained in English (€5, cash only, March-Oct daily 10:00-19:00, Nov-Feb Sat-Sun until 17:00 in winter, tel. 0185-267-101, www.castellobrown.com).

Or you could stroll the hilly pedestrian promenade through the trees from Portofino to **Paraggi beach,** and, if you're lucky, see a wild boar en route (20 minutes, path starts to the right of yellow-and-gray-striped Divo Martino church—look for clock tower, parallels main road, ends at ritzy Paraggi beach, where it's easy to catch bus back to Santa Margherita Ligure).

Another option is to hike out to **San Fruttuoso Abbey** and the nearby underwater Christ statue (described next; the hike there is steep at beginning and end, takes about 2.5 hours from Portofino—pick up the trailhead at the inland-most point of town, past Piazza della Libertà and the *carabinieri* station; you can also hike all the way there from Santa Margherita in about 4.5 hours via Portofino).

The **Parco di Portofino** can provide more information on the many hiking trails that crisscross Portofino's regional parklands (tel. 0185 289-479, www.parcoportofino.it).

NEAR PORTOFINO

San Fruttuoso Abbey
(Abbazia di San Fruttuoso)

This 11th-century abbey is accessible only by foot (a 2.5-hour hike from Portofino, 4 hours from Santa Margherita) or boat (from either Portofino, Santa Margherita, or Camogli; abbey entry-€5; June-Sept daily 10:00-17:45; shorter hours offseason and closed Mon in winter; last entry 45 minutes before closing, tel. 0185-772-703, www.fondoambiente.it). But the abbey itself isn't the main attraction. The

RIVIERA TOWNS

more intriguing draw is 60 feet underwater, offshore from the abbey, in a specially protected marine area: the statue *Christ of the Abyss (Cristo degli Abissi)*. A boat will take you out to a spot above the statue, where you can look down to just barely see the arms of Jesus—outstretched, reaching upward. Some people bring goggles and dive in for a better view. The statue was placed there in 1954 for the divine protection of the region's divers (€6, trips depart from San Fruttuoso July-Aug Sat at 15:30, some Mon and Wed sailings—check schedule at www.sopraesottoilmare.net or ask at Portofino TI).

Getting There: The same boats that link Santa Margherita Ligure and Portofino continue on to the San Fruttuoso Abbey (schedule at www.traghettiportofino.it). From Easter through September, a different company's boats continue north from the abbey to Camogli (train station), Recco, and Punta Chiappa (€5-8 one-way, can return to Santa Margherita by train from Camogli or buy round-trip boat tickets, tel. 0185-772-091, schedule at www.golfoparadiso.it). For details inquire at the TI in Portofino or Santa Margherita.

South of the Cinque Terre

La Spezia

While just a quick train ride away from the fanciful Cinque Terre (20-30 minutes), the working town of La Spezia feels like "reality Italy." Primarily a jumping-off point for travelers, the town is slim on sights, and has no beaches.

The pedestrian zone on Via del Prione to the gardens along the harbor makes a pleasant stroll. The nearly deserted **Museo Amedeo Lia** displays Italian paintings from the 13th to 18th century, including minor works by Venetian masters Titian, Tintoretto, and Canaletto (€7, Tue-Sun 10:00-18:00, closed Mon, audioguide-€3, 10-minute walk from station at Via del Prione 234, tel. 0187-731-100, museolia.spezianet.it).

Stay in the Cinque Terre if you can. But if you're in a bind, I've listed several La Spezia accommodations. I've also listed (under "Eating in La Spezia") some places to grab a meal while you wait for a train.

Orientation to La Spezia

Tourist Information: The **Cinque Terre National Park** office is on the platform at track 1—facing the tracks, go right (daily 7:30-19:30, off-season 9:00-17:30, tel. 0187-743-500, www.parconazionale5terre.it). Inside the station, to the right of the ticket counter, is the **La Spezia/Portovenere TI** (daily April-Oct 9:30-13:00 & 14:00-18:00, until 16:00 off-season).

ARRIVAL IN LA SPEZIA

By Train: Get off at the La Spezia Centrale stop. You can check your bags at the train station (see "Helpful Hints," next). Exit the station down the road to the left, where several recommended hotels and eateries are located. Another exit takes you out onto Via Fiume by way of the parking garage.

By Car: A handy parking option is under the train station, at the **Park Centro Stazione** (enter from Via Fiume; €6/half-day, about €17/day, tel. 0187-187-5303, www.mobpark.eu). You can park for free at **Piazza d'Armi**—look for the entrance at Via XV Giugno 1918 (20-minute walk to station).

HELPFUL HINTS

Market Days: A colorful covered market sets up in Piazza Cavour (Mon-Sat 7:00-13:00). On Fridays, a huge all-day open-air market sprawls along Viale Garibaldi, about six blocks from the station.

Baggage Storage: A left-luggage service is at the train station along track 1 (next to the WC). It's secure, though it isn't always staffed—ring the bell to call the attendant (€3/12 hours, daily 8:00-22:00, they'll photocopy your ID).

Laundry: A handy self-service launderette is just below the train station. Head down toward town, and immediately at the first piazza take a sharp right on Via Fiume—it's at #95 (one-hour wash and dry-€8, daily 8:30-20:30, mobile 320-055-6968).

Booking Agency: Cinque Terre Riviera books rooms and apartments in La Spezia, the Cinque Terre, and Portovenere for a 10 percent markup.

Getting to the Cinque Terre: Trains leave about twice hourly for the Cinque Terre, though not all trains stop at all towns. The Cinque Terre Treno Multi-Service Card (covers train ride to Cinque Terre as well as hiking fee) is sold at the train-station ticket window and at the national park office in the station. It's also possible to take boat excursions to the Cinque Terre, Portovenere, and outer islands from the La Spezia dock; for current schedules, check at the TI, dock, or www.navigazionegolfodeipoeti.it.

RIVIERA TOWNS

Sleeping in La Spezia

Sleep in La Spezia only as a last resort. These hotels and rooms are within a five-minute walk of La Spezia's station—except the last two listings, which work well for drivers only. Prices listed are high-season rates.

HOTELS

$$$ Hotel Firenze e Continentale is grand and Old World, but newly restored with a mountain-view breakfast room to boot. Just to the left of the station, its 68 rooms have all the usual comforts (prices generally, Db-€170-180, email for best rate, 10 percent direct booking discount off their best rate with this book, cheaper during slow times, air-con, elevator, garage parking-€22/day, Via Paleocapa 7, tel. 0187-713-200 or 0187-713-210, www.hotelfirenzecontinentale.it, info@hotelfirenzecontinentale.it).

$$ Hotel Astoria, with 47 simply furnished rooms, has a combination lobby and breakfast room as large as a school cafeteria (older Db without air-con-€80; Db-€95 for the 10 summery, mod-

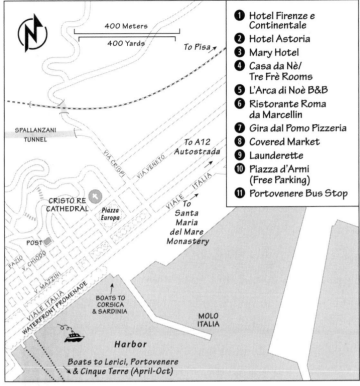

● Hotel Firenze e Continentale
● Hotel Astoria
● Mary Hotel
● Casa da Nè/ Tre Frè Rooms
● L'Arca di Noè B&B
● Ristorante Roma da Marcellin
● Gira dal Pomo Pizzeria
● Covered Market
● Launderette
● Piazza d'Armi (Free Parking)
● Portovenere Bus Stop

ern "superior" rooms with air-con; elevator to some rooms, take Via Milano left of Albergo Parma, go 3 blocks, and turn left to reach Via Roma 139; tel. 0187-714-655, www.albergoastoria.com, info@albergoastoria.com).

$$ Mary Hotel, directly across from the train station, has 48 basic rooms above a big lounge/game room (Sb-€68, Db-€100, air-con, elevator, Via Fiume 177, tel. 0187-743-254, www.hotelmary.it, info@hotelmary.it, friendly Luca).

PRIVATE ROOMS

Affitta camera—guesthouses or rented rooms with no official reception—abound near the station. Expect good deals and modest English skills.

$$ Casa da Nè/Tre Frè has 14 chic rooms with comfy linens and orange trees outside the door. It's located so close to the station that some rooms look out at the tracks; luckily, the windows are double-paned (Db-€80, Tb-€100, Qb-€120, includes breakfast at a café, air-con, Via Paleocapa 4, mobile 347-351-3239, www.trefre.it, info@trefre.it, Paolo).

$$ L'Arca di Noè B&B is homey, with three bright and artsy rooms at a great price (two have a bathroom inside the room, while the other has a private bathroom down the hall). A group could take the entire massive apartment (D-€60, Tb-€90, cash only, includes breakfast, air-con, communal kitchen, 5-minute walk from station at Via Fiume 39, mobile 320-485-2434, montialessandra@email.it, Alessandra).

NEAR LA SPEZIA

$$ Il Gelsomino, for drivers only, is a homey B&B in the hills above La Spezia overlooking the Gulf of Poets. It has three tranquil rooms (Db-€70, Tb-€90, Qb-€110, reconfirm several days in advance with your arrival time, Via dei Viseggi 9, tel. 0187-704-201, www.ilgelsomino.biz, ilgelsomino@inwind.it, gracious Carla and Walter Massi).

$ Santa Maria del Mare Monastery, rents 15 comfortable rooms to spiritual travelers high above La Spezia in a scenic but institutional setting (recommended donation: dorm bed-€35, Db-€60, includes breakfast, additional €15/person for a meal, Via Montalbano 135B, tel. 0187-711-332, mobile 347-848-3993, www.santamariadelmare.it, madre@santamariadelmare.191.it).

Eating in La Spezia

Ristorante Roma da Marcellin, just down from the station, has a cool, leafy terrace that's ideal for relaxing while you await your train. Grandpa Ottorino cooks up the freshest catch, as well as homemade ravioli and spaghetti *frutti di mare* (€8-12 pastas, €10-15 *secondi*, daily; as you exit the station, turn left—it's across from Hotel Firenze e Continentale at Via Paleocapa 18; tel. 0187-715-921).

Gira dal Pomo Pizzeria, just a few doors farther down on the corner of Via Zampino, offers more reasonable prices and an extensive selection of €5-8 pizzas and pastas (closed Sun, Piazza S. Bon 5, tel. 0187-301-284).

La Spezia Connections

From La Spezia by Train to: Monterosso (2-3/hour, 15-30 minutes), **Carrara** (2/hour, 25 minutes), **Viareggio** (2/hour, 30-60 minutes), **Pisa** (about hourly, 1-1.5 hours), **Florence** (5/day direct, 2.5 hours, otherwise nearly hourly with change in Pisa), **Rome** (8/day direct, more with transfers in Pisa, 3-4.5 hours), **Milan** (about hourly, 3 hours direct or with change in Genoa), **Venice** (about hourly, 5-6 hours, 1-3 changes).

By Bus to Portovenere: City buses generally depart from Viale Garibaldi (bus #P, 2/hour, 30 minutes, €2.50 each way; bus

#11 also makes this trip, but only mid-June–mid-Sept; buy tickets at TI, tobacco shops or newsstands). From the La Spezia train station, exit left and head downhill, following the street to the first square (Piazza S. Bon). Continue down the pedestrian stretch of Via Fiume to Piazza Garibaldi, then turn right at the fountain in the square onto Viale Garibaldi; the bus stop for Portovenere-bound buses is after the first stoplight on the right side of the street.

Carrara

What are perhaps the world's most famous marble quarries are just east of La Spezia in Carrara. Michelangelo himself traveled to these

valleys to pick out the marble that he would work into his masterpieces. The towns of the region are dominated by marble. The quarries higher up are vast digs that dwarf the hardworking trucks and machinery coming and going. The **Marble Museum** (Museo Civico del Marmo) traces the story of marble-cutting here from pre-Roman times until today (€5, May-Sept Mon-Sat 9:30-13:00 & 15:30-18:00, Oct-April Mon-Sat 9:00-12:30 & 14:30-17:00, closed Sun year-round, Viale XX Settembre 85, tel. 0585-845-746, www.museodelmarmo.com).

For a guided visit, **Sara Paolini** is excellent (€80/half-day tour, mobile 373-711-6695, sarapaolini@hotmail.com). Sara is accustomed to meeting drivers at the Carrara freeway exit, or she can pick you up at the train station.

Portovenere

While the gritty port of La Spezia offers little in the way of redeeming touristic value, the nearby resort of Portovenere is enchanting. This Cinque Terre-esque village clings to a rocky promontory that juts into the sea and protects the harbor from the crashing waves. On the harbor, next to colorful bobbing boats, a row of restaurants—perfect for al fresco dining—feature local specialties such as *trenette* pasta with pesto and *spaghetti con frutti di mare*.

Local boats take you on a 40-minute excursion around three nearby islands or over to Lerici, the town across the bay. Lord Byron swam to Lerici (not recommended). Hardy hikers enjoy the

five-hour (or more) hike to Riomaggiore, the nearest Cinque Terre town.

Getting There: Portovenere—not to be confused with Portofino—is an easy day trip from the Cinque Terre by **boat** (mid-June-Oct, 4/day, 1 hour, €13 one-way, €25 day pass includes hopping on and off and either Lerici or a jaunt around three small islands near Portovenere, www.navigazionegolfodeipoeti.it). You can also cruise between Portovenere and Santa Margherita Ligure, with stops in Vernazza and Sestri Levante, using another boat line (www.traghettiportofino.it). Or you can take the **bus** from La Spezia (bus #P, 2/hour, 30 minutes, €2.50 each way; bus #11 also makes this trip, but only mid-June-mid-Sept and off-season Sat; in La Spezia buy tickets at tobacco shops or newsstands; in Portovenere get tickets at TI). **Parking** is a nightmare here from May through September. In peak season, buses shuttle drivers from the parking lot just outside Portovenere to the harborside square. Otherwise, test your luck with the spots on the seaside (€2/hour).

Tourist Information: The TI is easy to find in the main square (June-Sept daily 10:00-12:00 & 15:00-19:45, Oct-May shorter hours and closed Wed, Piazza Bastreri 7, tel. 0187-790-691, www.prolocoportovenere.it).

Sleeping in Portovenere: If you've forgotten your yacht, try **$$ Albergo Il Genio,** in the building where the main street hits the piazza (Db-€100, Qb-€130, some rooms with views, no elevator, free parking—request when you reserve, Piazza Bastreri 8, tel. 0187-790-611, www.hotelgenioportovenere.com, info@hotelgenioportovenere.com).

PRACTICALITIES

This section covers just the basics on traveling in Italy (for much more information, see *Rick Steves Italy*). You'll find free advice on specific topics at www.ricksteves.com/tips.

MONEY

Italy uses the euro currency: 1 euro (€) = about $1.10. To convert prices in euros to dollars, add about 10 percent: €20 = about $22, €50 = about $55. (Check www.oanda.com for the latest exchange rates.)

The standard way for travelers to get euros is to withdraw money from ATMs (which locals call a *bancomat*) using a debit or credit card, ideally with a Visa or MasterCard logo. Before departing, call your bank or credit-card company: Confirm that your card(s) will work overseas, ask about international transaction fees, and alert them that you'll be making withdrawals in Europe. Also ask for the PIN number for your credit card in case it'll help you use Europe's "chip-and-PIN" payment machines (see below); allow time for your bank to mail your PIN to you. To keep your valuables safe while traveling, wear a money belt.

Dealing with "Chip and PIN": Much of Europe (including Italy) is adopting a "chip-and-PIN" system for credit cards, and some merchants rely on it exclusively. European chip-and-PIN cards are embedded with an electronic chip, in addition to the magnetic stripe used on our American-style cards. This means that your credit (and debit) card might not work at payment machines, such as those at train and subway stations, toll roads, parking garages, luggage lockers, and gas pumps. Major US banks are beginning to offer credit cards with chips, but many of these are chip-and-signature cards, for which your signature (not your PIN) verifies your identity. In Europe, these cards should work for live transactions and at most payment machines, but probably won't work for offline transactions such as at unattended gas pumps. If a payment machine won't take your card, look for a machine that takes cash or see if there's a cashier nearby who can manually process your transaction. Often the easiest solution is to pay for your purchases with cash you've withdrawn from an ATM using your debit card (Europe's ATMs still accept magnetic-stripe cards).

Dynamic Currency Conversion: If merchants or hoteliers offer to convert your purchase price into dollars (called dynamic currency conversion, or DCC), refuse this "service." You'll pay more in fees for the expensive convenience of seeing your charge in dollars. If an ATM offers to "lock in" or "guarantee" your conversion rate, choose "proceed without conversion." Other prompts might state, "You can be charged in dollars: Press YES for dollars, NO for euros." Always choose the local currency.

STAYING CONNECTED

Smart travelers call ahead or go online to double-check tourist information, learn the latest on sights (special events, tour schedules, and so on), book tickets and tours, make reservations, reconfirm hotels, and research transportation connections.

To call Italy from the US or Canada: Dial 011-39 and then the local number. (The 011 is our international access code, and 39 is Italy's country code.)

To call Italy from a European country: Dial 00-39 followed by the local number. (The 00 is Europe's international access code.)

To call within Italy: Just dial the local number.

To call from Italy to another country: Dial 00 followed by the country code (for example, 1 for the US or Canada), then the area code and number. If you're calling European countries whose phone numbers begin with 0, you'll usually omit that 0 when you dial.

Tips: Traveling with a mobile phone—whether an American one that works in Italy, or a European one you buy when you arrive—is handy, but can be pricey. Consider getting an international plan; most providers offer a global calling plan that cuts the per-minute cost of phone calls and texts, and a flat-fee data plan.

Use Wi-Fi whenever possible. Most hotels and many cafés offer free Wi-Fi, and you'll likely also find it at tourist information offices, major museums, and public-transit hubs. With Wi-Fi you can use your smartphone to make free or inexpensive domestic and international calls by taking advantage of a calling app such as Skype, FaceTime, or Google+ Hangouts. When you can't find Wi-Fi, you can use your cellular network to connect to the Internet, text, or make voice calls. When you're done, avoid further charges by manually switching off "data roaming" or "cellular data."

It's possible to stay connected without a mobile phone. To make cheap international calls from any phone (even your hotel-room

From:	rick@ricksteves.com
Sent:	Today
To:	info@hotelcentral.com
Subject:	Reservation request for 19-22 July

Dear Hotel Central,

I would like to reserve a double room for 2 people for 3 nights, arriving 19 July and departing 22 July. If possible, I would like a quiet room with a bathroom inside the room.

Please let me know if you have a room available and the price.

Thank you!
Rick Steves

phone), you can buy an international phone card in Italy. These work with a scratch-to-reveal PIN code, allow you to call home to the US for pennies a minute, and also work for domestic calls. Calling from your hotel-room phone without using an international phone card is usually expensive. Though they are disappearing in Italy, you can still find public pay phones in post offices and train stations. For more on phoning, see www.ricksteves.com/phoning.

MAKING HOTEL RESERVATIONS

I recommend reserving rooms in advance, particularly during peak season. For the best rates, book directly with the hotel using their official website (not a booking agency's site). If there's no secure reservation form, or for complicated requests, send an email with the following information: number and type of rooms; number of nights; arrival date; departure date; and any special requests. (For a sample email, see the sidebar.) Use the European style for writing dates: day/month/year. Hoteliers typically ask for your credit-card number as a deposit.

Some hotels are willing to deal to attract guests—try emailing several to ask their best price. In general, hotel prices can soften if you do any of the following: offer to pay cash, stay at least three nights, or travel off-season. You can also try asking for a cheaper room or a discount.

While most taxes are included in the price, a variable city tax of €1.50-5/person per night is often added to hotel bills in Italy (and is not included in the prices in this book). Some hoteliers will ask to collect the city tax in cash to make their bookkeeping and accounting simpler.

EATING

Italy offers a wide array of eateries. A *ristorante* is a formal restaurant, while a *trattoria* or *osteria* is usually more traditional and simpler (but can still be pricey). Italian "bars" are not taverns, but small cafés selling sandwiches, coffee, and other drinks. An *enoteca* is a wine bar with snacks and light meals. Take-away food from pizza shops and delis (*rosticcería*) makes an easy picnic.

Italians eat dinner a bit later than we do; better restaurants start serving around 19:00. A full meal consists of an appetizer (antipasto), a first course (*primo piatto*, pasta, rice, or soup), and a second course (*secondo piatto*, expensive meat and fish/seafood dishes). Vegetables *(verdure)* may come with the *secondo*, but more often must be ordered separately as a side dish (*contorno*). Desserts (*dolci*) can be very tempting. The euros can add up in a hurry, but you don't have to order each course. My approach is to mix antipasti and *primi piatti* family-style with my dinner partners (skipping *secondi*). Or, for a basic value, look for a *menù del giorno*, a three- or four-course, fixed-price meal deal (avoid the cheapest ones, often called a *menù turistico*).

Good service is relaxed (slow to an American). You won't get the bill until you ask for it: *"Il conto?"* Most restaurants include a service charge in their prices (check the menu for *servizio incluso*—generally around 10 percent). You can add on a tip, if you choose, by including a euro or two for each person in your party. If you order at a counter rather than from waitstaff, there's no need to tip. Many (but not all) restaurants in Italy add a cover charge *(coperto)* of €1-3.50 per person to your bill.

At bars and cafés, getting a drink while standing at the bar (*banco)* is cheaper than drinking it at a table *(tavolo)* or sitting outside *(terrazza)*. This tiered pricing system is clearly posted on the wall. Sometimes you'll pay at a cash register, then take the receipt to another counter to claim your drink.

TRANSPORTATION

By Train: In Italy, most travelers find it's cheapest simply to buy train tickets as they go. To see if a railpass could save you money, check www.ricksteves.com/rail. To research train schedules, visit Germany's excellent all-Europe website, www.bahn.com, or Italy's www.trenitalia.com. A private company called Italo also runs fast trains on major routes in Italy; see www.italotreno.it.

You can buy tickets at train stations (at the ticket window or at machines with English instructions) or from travel agencies. Before boarding the train, you must validate your train documents by stamping them in the machine near the platform (usually marked *convalida biglietti* or *vidimazione*). Strikes *(sciopero)* are common and generally announced in advance (but a few sporadic trains still run—ask around).

By Car: It's cheaper to arrange most car rentals from the US. For tips on your insurance options, see www.ricksteves.com/

cdw, and for route planning, consult www.viamichelin.com. Theft insurance is mandatory in Italy ($15-20/day). In Italy, most car-rental companies' rates automatically include Collision Damage Waiver (CDW) coverage. Even if you try to decline CDW when you reserve your Italian car, you may find when you show up at the counter that you must buy it after all.

Bring your driver's license. You're also technically required to have an International Driving Permit (sold at your local AAA office for $15 plus the cost of two passport-type photos; see www.aaa.com).

Italy's superhighway *(autostrada)* system is slick and speedy, but you'll pay a toll. Be warned that car traffic is restricted in many city centers—don't drive or park in any area that has a sign reading *Zona Traffico Limitato* (*ZTL,* often shown above a red circle)...or you might be mailed a ticket later.

Italians love to tailgate; otherwise, local road etiquette is similar to that in the US. Ask your car-rental company for details, or check the US State Department website (www.travel.state.gov, click on "International Travel," then specify your country of choice and click "Traffic Safety and Road Conditions").

A car is a worthless headache in cities—park it safely (get tips from your hotelier). As break-ins are common, be sure all of your valuables are out of sight and locked in the trunk, or even better, with you or in your hotel room.

HELPFUL HINTS

Emergency Help: For English-speaking **police** help, dial 113. To summon an **ambulance**, call 118. For passport problems, call the **US Embassy** (in Rome, 24-hour line—tel. 06-46741) or **US Consulates** (Milan—tel. 02-290-351, Florence—tel. 055-266-951, Naples—tel. 081-583-8111); or the **Canadian Embassy** (in Rome, tel. 06-854-442-911). If you have a minor illness, do as the locals do and go to a pharmacist for advice. Or ask at your hotel for help—they'll know of the nearest medical and emergency services. For other concerns, get advice from your hotelier.

Theft or Loss: Italy has particularly hardworking pickpockets—wear a money belt. Assume beggars are pickpockets and any scuffle is simply a distraction by a team of thieves. If you stop for any commotion or show, put your hands in your pockets before someone else does.

To replace a passport, you'll need to go in person to an embassy or consulate (see above). Cancel and replace your credit and debit cards by calling these 24-hour US numbers collect: Visa—tel. 303/967-1096, MasterCard—tel. 636/722-7111, American Express—tel. 336/393-1111. In Italy, to make a collect call to the US, dial 800-172-444; press zero or stay on the line for an operator.

File a police report either on the spot or within a day or two; you'll need it to submit an insurance claim for lost or stolen railpasses or electronics, and it can help with replacing your passport or credit and debit cards. Precautionary measures can minimize the effects of loss—back up your digital photos and other files frequently. For more information, see www.ricksteves.com/help.

Time: Italy uses the 24-hour clock. It's the same through 12:00 noon, then keep going: 13:00, 14:00, and so on. Italy, like most of continental Europe, is six/nine hours ahead of the East/West Coasts of the US.

Business Hours: Many businesses have now adopted the government's recommended 8:00 to 14:00 workday (although in tourist areas, shops are open longer). Still, expect small towns and villages to be more or less shut tight during the midafternoon. Stores are also usually closed on Sunday, and often on Monday.

Sights: Opening and closing hours of sights can change unexpectedly; confirm the latest times with the local tourist information office or its website. Some major churches enforce a modest dress code (no bare shoulders or shorts) for everyone, even children.

Holidays and Festivals: Italy celebrates many holidays, which can close sights and attract crowds (book hotel rooms ahead). For information on holidays and festivals, check Italy's website: www.italia.it. For a simple list showing major—though not all—events, see www.ricksteves.com/festivals.

Numbers and Stumblers: What Americans call the second floor of a building is the first floor in Europe. Europeans write dates as day/month/year, so Christmas 2016 is 25/12/16. Commas are decimal points and vice versa—a dollar and a half is 1,50, and there are 5.280 feet in a mile. Italy uses the metric system: A kilogram is 2.2 pounds; a liter is about a quart; and a kilometer is six-tenths of a mile.

RESOURCES FROM RICK STEVES

This Snapshot guide is excerpted from my latest edition of *Rick Steves Italy*, which is one of more than 30 titles in my series of guidebooks on European travel. I also produce a public television series, *Rick Steves' Europe*, and a public radio show, *Travel with Rick Steves*. My website, www.ricksteves.com, offers free travel information, a forum for travelers' comments, guidebook updates, my travel blog, an online travel store, and information on European railpasses and our tours of Europe. If you're bringing a mobile device on your trip, you can download my free Rick Steves Audio Europe app, featuring podcasts of my radio shows, audio tours of major sights in Europe, and travel interviews about Italy. You can get Rick Steves Audio Europe via Apple's App Store, Google

Play, or the Amazon Appstore. For more information, see www.
ricksteves.com/audioeurope. You can also follow me on Facebook
and Twitter.

ADDITIONAL RESOURCES
Tourist Information: www.italia.it
Passports and Red Tape: www.travel.state.gov
Packing List: www.ricksteves.com/packing
Travel Insurance: www.ricksteves.com/insurance
Cheap Flights: www.kayak.com
Airplane Carry-on Restrictions: www.tsa.gov
Updates for This Book: www.ricksteves.com/update

How Was Your Trip?
If you'd like to share your tips, concerns, and discoveries after
using this book, please fill out the survey at www.ricksteves.com/
feedback. Thanks in advance—it helps a lot.

PRACTICALITIES

Italian Survival Phrases

English	Italian	Pronunciation
Good day.	*Buon giorno.*	bwohn **jor**-noh
Do you speak English?	*Parla inglese?*	**par**-lah een-**glay**-zay
Yes. / No.	*Sì. / No.*	see / noh
I (don't) understand.	*(Non) capisco.*	(nohn) kah-**pees**-koh
Please.	*Per favore.*	pehr fah-**voh**-ray
Thank you.	*Grazie.*	**graht**-seeay
You're welcome.	*Prego.*	**pray**-go
I'm sorry.	*Mi dispiace.*	mee dee-speeah-chay
Excuse me.	*Mi scusi.*	mee **skoo**-zee
(No) problem.	*(Non) c'è un problema.*	(nohn) cheh oon proh-**blay**-mah
Good.	*Va bene.*	vah **behn**-ay
Goodbye.	*Arrivederci.*	ah-ree-vay-**dehr**-chee
one / two	*uno / due*	**oo**-noh / **doo**-ay
three / four	*tre / quattro*	tray / **kwah**-troh
five / six	*cinque / sei*	**cheeng**-kway / **seh**ee
seven / eight	*sette / otto*	**seht**-tay / **ot**-toh
nine / ten	*nove / dieci*	**nov**-ay / **deeay**-chee
How much is it?	*Quanto costa?*	**kwahn**-toh **kos**-tah
Write it?	*Me lo scrive?*	may loh **skree**-vay
Is it free?	*È gratis?*	eh **grah**-tees
Is it included?	*È incluso?*	eh een-**kloo**-zoh
Where can I buy / find...?	*Dove posso comprare / trovare...?*	**doh**-vay **pos**-soh kohm-**prah**-ray / troh-**vah**-ray
I'd like / We'd like...	*Vorrei / Vorremmo...*	vor-**rehe**e / vor-**ray**-moh
...a room.	*...una camera.*	**oo**-nah **kah**-meh-rah
...a ticket to ____.	*...un biglietto per ____.*	oon beel-**yeht**-toh pehr
Is it possible?	*È possibile?*	eh poh-**see**-bee-lay
Where is...?	*Dov'è...?*	**doh**-veh
...the train station	*...la stazione*	lah staht-see**oh**-nay
...the bus station	*...la stazione degli autobus*	lah staht-see**oh**-nay **dayl**-yee **ow**-toh-boos
...tourist information	*...informazioni per turisti*	een-for-maht-see**oh**-nee pehr too-**ree**-stee
...the toilet	*...la toilette*	lah twah-**leht**-tay
men	*uomini, signori*	**woh**-mee-nee, seen-**yoh**-ree
women	*donne, signore*	**don**-nay, seen-**yoh**-ray
left / right	*sinistra / destra*	see-**nee**-strah / **dehs**-trah
straight	*sempre diritto*	**sehm**-pray dee-**ree**-toh
When do you open / close?	*A che ora aprite / chiudete?*	ah kay **oh**-rah ah-**pree**-tay / keeoo-**day**-tay
At what time?	*A che ora?*	ah kay **oh**-rah
Just a moment.	*Un momento.*	oon moh-**mayn**-toh
now / soon / later	*adesso / presto / tardi*	ah-**dehs**-soh / **prehs**-toh / **tar**-dee
today / tomorrow	*oggi / domani*	**oh**-jee / doh-**mah**-nee

In an Italian-speaking Restaurant

English	Italian	Pronunciation
I'd like...	Vorrei...	vor-**rehee**
We'd like...	Vorremmo...	vor-**ray**-moh
...to reserve...	...prenotare...	pray-noh-**tah**-ray
...a table for one / two.	...un tavolo per uno / due.	oon **tah**-voh-loh pehr **oo**-noh / **doo**-ay
Non-smoking.	Non fumare.	nohn foo-**mah**-ray
Is this seat free?	È libero questo posto?	eh **lee**-bay-roh **kwehs**-toh **poh**-stoh
The menu (in English), please.	Il menù (in inglese), per favore.	eel may-**noo** (een een-**glay**-zay) pehr fah-**voh**-ray
service (not) included	servizio (non) incluso	sehr-**veet**-seeoh (nohn) een-**kloo**-zoh
cover charge	pane e coperto	**pah**-nay ay koh-**pehr**-toh
to go	da portar via	dah **por**-tar **vee**-ah
with / without	con / senza	kohn / **sehn**-sah
and / or	e / o	ay / oh
menu (of the day)	menù (del giorno)	may-**noo** (dayl **jor**-noh)
specialty of the house	specialità della casa	spay-chah-lee-**tah dehl**-lah **kah**-zah
first course (pasta, soup)	primo piatto	**pree**-moh peeah-toh
main course (meat, fish)	secondo piatto	say-**kohn**-doh peeah-toh
side dishes	contorni	kohn-**tor**-nee
bread	pane	**pah**-nay
cheese	formaggio	for-**mah**-joh
sandwich	panino	pah-**nee**-noh
soup	minestra, zuppa	mee-**nehs**-trah, **tsoo**-pah
salad	insalata	een-sah-**lah**-tah
meat	carne	**kar**-nay
chicken	pollo	**poh**-loh
fish	pesce	**peh**-shay
seafood	frutti di mare	**froo**-tee dee **mah**-ray
fruit / vegetables	frutta / legumi	**froo**-tah / lay-**goo**-mee
dessert	dolci	**dohl**-chee
tap water	acqua del rubinetto	**ah**-kwah dayl roo-bee-**nay**-toh
mineral water	acqua minerale	**ah**-kwah mee-nay-**rah**-lay
milk	latte	**lah**-tay
(orange) juice	succo (d'arancia)	**soo**-koh (dah-**rahn**-chah)
coffee / tea	caffè / tè	kah-**feh** / teh
wine	vino	**vee**-noh
red / white	rosso / bianco	**roh**-soh / bee**ahn**-koh
glass / bottle	bicchiere / bottiglia	bee-kee**ay**-ray / boh-**teel**-yah
beer	birra	**bee**-rah
Cheers!	Cin cin!	cheen cheen
More. / Another.	Ancora un po'. / Un altro.	ahn-**koh**-rah oon poh / oon **ahl**-troh
The same.	Lo stesso.	loh **stehs**-soh
The bill, please.	Il conto, per favore.	eel **kohn**-toh pehr fah-**voh**-ray
tip	mancia	**mahn**-chah
Delicious!	Delizioso!	day-leet-see**oh**-zoh

For more user-friendly Italian phrases, check out *Rick Steves' Italian Phrase Book & Dictionary* or *Rick Steves' French, Italian, and German Phrase Book*.

PRACTICALITIES

INDEX

INDEX

INDEX

Start your trip at

Our website enhances this book and turns

Explore Europe

At ricksteves.com you can browse through thousands of articles, videos, photos and radio interviews, plus find a wealth of money-saving travel tips for planning your dream trip. And with our mobile-friendly website, you can easily access all this great travel information anywhere you go.

TV Shows

Preview the places you'll visit by watching entire half-hour episodes of Rick Steves' Europe (choose from all 100 shows) on-demand, for free.

ricksteves.com

your travel dreams into affordable reality

Radio Interviews

Enjoy ready access to Rick's vast library of radio interviews covering travel

tips and cultural insights that relate specifically to your Europe travel plans.

Travel Forums

Learn, ask, share! Our online community of savvy travelers is a great resource for first-time travelers to Europe, as well as seasoned pros. You'll find forums on each country, plus travel tips and restaurant/hotel reviews. You can even ask one of our well-traveled staff to chime in with an opinion.

Travel News

Subscribe to our free Travel News e-newsletter, and get monthly updates from Rick on what's happening in Europe.

Rick's Free Travel App

Get your FREE **Rick Steves Audio Europe**™ app to enjoy…

- Dozens of self-guided tours of Europe's top museums, sights and historic walks
- Hundreds of tracks filled with cultural insights and sightseeing tips from Rick's radio interviews
- All organized into handy geographic playlists
- For iPhone, iPad, iPod Touch, Android

With Rick whispering in your ear, Europe gets even better.

Find out more at ricksteves.com

Gear up for your next adventure at ricksteves.com

Light Luggage

Pack light and right with Rick Steves' affordable, custom-designed rolling carry-on bags, backpacks, day packs and shoulder bags.

Accessories

From packing cubes to moneybelts and beyond, Rick has personally selected the travel goodies that will help your trip go smoother.

Save time and energy

This guidebook is your independent-travel toolkit. But for all it delivers, it's still up to you to devote the time and energy it takes to manage the preparation and logistics that are essential for a happy trip. If that's a hassle, there's a solution.

Rick Steves Tours

A Rick Steves tour takes you to Europe's most interesting places with great

with minimum stress

guides and small groups of 28 or less. We follow Rick's favorite itineraries, ride in comfy buses, stay in family-run hotels, and bring you intimately close to the Europe you've traveled so far to see. Most importantly, we take away the logistical headaches so you can focus on the fun.

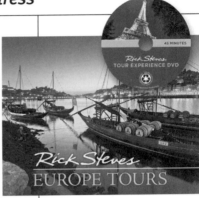

customers—along with us on 40 different itineraries, from Ireland to Italy to Istanbul. Is a Rick Steves tour the right fit for your travel dreams? Find out at ricksteves.com, where you can also get Rick's latest tour catalog and free Tour Experience DVD.

Join the fun

This year we'll take 18,000 free-spirited travelers— nearly half of them repeat

Europe is best experienced with happy travel partners. We hope you can join us.

See our itineraries at ricksteves.com

Rick Steves

Nearly all Rick Steves guides are available as ebooks. Check with your favorite bookseller.
Rick Steves guidebooks are published by Avalon Travel, a member of the Perseus Books Group.

Maximize your travel skills with a good guidebook.

Photo © Patricia Feaster

Avalon Travel
An imprint of Perseus Books
A Hachette Book Group company
1700 Fourth Street
Berkeley, CA 94710

Printed in Canada by Friesens
Second printing August 2016

ISBN 978-1-63121-201-7

For the latest on Rick's lectures, guidebooks, tours, public radio show, and public television series, contact Rick Steves' Europe, Inc., 130 Fourth Avenue North, Edmonds, WA 98020, tel. 425/771-8303, www.ricksteves.com, rick@ricksteves.com.

Rick Steves' Europe
Special Publications Manager: Risa Laib
Managing Editor: Jennifer Madison Davis
Editors: Glenn Eriksen, Tom Griffin, Katherine Gustafson, Suzanne Kotz, Cathy Lu, John Pierce, Carrie Shepherd
Editorial & Production Assistant: Jessica Shaw
Editorial Intern: Shirley Qiu
Researchers: Virginia Agostinelli, Ben Cameron, Trish Feaster, Cameron Hewitt, Suzanne Kotz
Contributor: Gene Openshaw
Maps & Graphics: David C. Hoerlein, Sandra Hundacker, Lauren Mills, Mary Rostad

Avalon Travel
Senior Editor and Series Manager: Madhu Prasher
Editor: Jamie Andrade
Associate Editor: Maggie Ryan
Copy Editors: Judith Brown and Suzie Nasol
Proofreader: Denise Silva
Indexer: Stephen Callahan
Production and Typesetting: Rue Flaherty, Tabitha Lahr
Cover Design: Kimberly Glyder Design
Maps & Graphics: Kat Bennett, Mike Morgenfeld

Photo Credits
Front Cover: Riomaggiore, Cinque Terre © Stefano Politi Markovina / Alamy Stock
Additional Photography: Dominic Arizona Bonuccelli, Ben Cameron, Julie Coen, Jennifer Hauseman, Cameron Hewitt, David C. Hoerlein, Gene Openshaw, Michael Potter, Robyn Stencil, Rick Steves, Bruce VanDeventer, Laura VanDeventer, Les Wahlstrom, Ian Watson, Tom Wallace, Wikimedia Commons (PD-Art/PD-US), Deanna Woodruff (photos are used by permission and are the property of the original copyright owners).